Puffin Books
Editor: Kaye Webb

THE PUFFIN BOOK OF FOOTBALLERS

Any one person's selection of the greatest footballers past and present is going to be individual and idiosyncratic. And what a mine of information this selection is. Brian Glanville, with his incomparable knowledge of the game, picks his greatest players and gives a brief biography of their lives and playing skills. The players span football from its beginnings to the present, and though it can in no way be described as an encyclopaedia, most of the great players are represented. They appear strictly alphabetically, so the greats of the 1920s stand beside the players of today, and the book as a whole gives a fascinating and impressionistic history of football and the great matches through the players themselves.

Brian Glanville

The Puffin Book of Footballers

Puffin Books

Puffin Books, Penguin Books Ltd, Harmondsworth,
Middlesex, England
Penguin Books, 625 Madison Avenue,
New York, New York 10022, U.S.A.
Penguin Books Australia Ltd, Ringwood,
Victoria, Australia
Penguin Books Canada Ltd, 2801 John Street,
Markham, Ontario, Canada L3R 1B4
Penguin Books (N.Z.) Ltd, 182–190 Wairau Road,
Auckland 10, New Zealand

Published in Puffin Books 1978
Copyright © Brian Glanville, 1978

All rights reserved

Made and printed in Great Britain by
Hazell Watson & Viney Ltd, Aylesbury, Bucks
Set in Linotype Times

Except in the United States of America, this
book is sold subject to the condition that
it shall not, by way of trade or otherwise, be lent,
re-sold, hired out, or otherwise circulated without
the publisher's prior consent in any form of
binding or cover other than that in which it is
published and without a similar condition
including this condition being imposed on the
subsequent purchaser

INTRODUCTION

Let me begin with an admission. A book of this kind, ranging from the origins of the game, nearly 100 years ago, to the heroes of today – from Lord Kinnaird to Cruyff, if you wish – spanning the world, containing some 200 short biographies, cannot claim to be comprehensive. It must be personal: if not arbitrary. I have put in the players *I* think should be included, the players who, taken together, not only stand out as the finest of their time, but give some idea of the development of the game. I have placed them side by side, rather than divide them into historical sections, because I think it is the easiest form of reference, and also because I hope it gives a feeling of organic growth. Cruyff, that is to say, would have been impossible without Kinnaird. Gilmar, the Brazilian goalkeeper, who once played for the Corinthians of Sao Paulo, was in a sense perpetuating the Corinthians of that perfect knight among centre-forwards, G. O. Smith, after whom his club was named.

Today's footballers one has had to take on trust. Time passes, time assesses, time revalues; but the book would be a poor companion if it did not give a panorama of football and footballers as they are now. In any case, football today seems to me astonishingly good; exciting and enterprising. The years of dull negativity, defence at all costs, seem to have rolled away, giving place to what we call, for want of a better word, Total Football; though as I point out in the text, such stars as Peter Doherty, in the thirties, Alfredo Di Stefano, in the fifties, were playing Total Football before it had been invented.

Each biography tries to convey something of a player's style, something of his career. The longer ago he played, the easier it is to gain a true perspective, the less relevant such criteria as international caps seem to be. Thus it is quite clear that three of the finest English footballers of the 1920s were Frank Barson, Jimmy Dimmock and Clem Stephenson; who scarcely played for England at all: a reflection on the selectors rather than themselves.

The great teams are, I hope, amply represented: Scotland's Wembley Wizards of 1928, Arsenal in the 1930s, Austria's Wunderteam of the same era (Arsenal beat it 4–2!), Real Madrid and Hungary of the 1950s, Brazil of 1958 and 1970, West Germany and Holland in still more recent years. As the game has grown, so more and more countries have made their distinguished contribution; and we have yet to see the best of Africa, with its myriad talents.

The book, then, is impressionistic rather than encyclopaedic. Most of the great players of the game's history should be found here; but greatness, after all, is itself a matter of opinion.

Julio Cesar Abbadie (Uruguay). He came, saw and conquered in the World Cup Finals of 1954 when he and his fellow winger, Borges, ripped Scotland's defence to pieces in Basel. Borges scored three of the goals, Abbadie two, the last a magnificent solo when he dribbled round both fullbacks and the goalkeeper. Abbadie was hurt playing against England in the quarter-finals, thus missing the semi-final, lost to Hungary in Lausanne. His presence might have made a great difference. Strongly built, very fast, a scintillating ball player, he was born in Montevideo on 7 September 1930. From the right wing he converted to inside-left, where he was just as successful, leaving the famous Penarol club in his native city in 1956 to play there for Genoa in the Italian Championship.

Marques Menezes Ademir (Brazil). The irresistible centre-forward of the dazzling Brazilian team which dominated the 1950 World Cup, until Uruguay beat them to win it, in Rio. Ademir, like his successor in the Brazilian national team, Vavà (q.v.), was born in Recife, the capital of Pernambuco, and, like Vavà, began with the Recife club. From there he moved to Rio's Fluminense and – again like Vavà – to Vasco da Gama, being a member of their unbeaten Championship team of 1949. Slim, dark, mobile and explosively quick, a master of the ball, he was leading scorer of the 1950 World Cup with seven goals. Afterwards, injuries marred his international career.

Florian Albert (Hungary). A centre-forward who was European Footballer of the Year in 1967, Albert, like all truly great players, excelled in a World Cup; that of 1966. His staggeringly versatile performance against Brazil in the rain at Everton, when he was at once orchestrator and executioner, led to an ovation from the English fans at the end. Thus he fully confirmed the promise he had shown when he won his first cap as a seventeen-year-old in 1958, and again in the Olympic Games tournament two years later, when he had a memorable partnership with Grosics. Succeeding Nandor Hidegkuti as Hungary's centre-forward was no easy matter, but Albert in his own fluent, elegant way was Hidegkuti's equal. Born in Budapest in 1940, his first World Cup was that of 1962 in Chile, when he scored a glorious individual goal against England in Rancagua, and followed that with a hat trick against the Bulgarians. Ferencvaros was his only major club and when he retired, he became a journalist. At his peak, he had speed, balance, breathtaking close control, and a strong right-footed shot.

Ivor Allchurch (Wales). Allchurch's record of sixty-seven Welsh international caps, thirty-seven in the British Championship, the rest against foreign opposition, will take some beating. A player who impressed from the moment he got into the Swansea Town team as a teenager, Allchurch's blond head, his exciting dribbling, his clever passing, all took the eye. Allchurch's splendid international career extended over seventeen years, beginning in season 1950–51 with Swansea, where he was born, ending in 1967–8 with Swansea again, the wheel come full circle, after he had spent four good years with Newcastle United and another two with Cardiff City. In 1958, he was a member of the gallant Welsh team which reached the quarter-finals of the Swedish World Cup against Brazil, and he himself scored their goal against Mexico. He played more than 600 League games, after his debut in 1949, and was deservedly awarded the MBE. His brother Len, a right winger, was also a Welsh international forward.

José Altafini (Brazil and Italy). A centre-forward of astounding longevity, leader of the Brazilian attack – till displaced by Vavà (q.v.) – in the 1958 World Cup at nineteen, a First Division player in Italy for the next eighteen years. Only in July 1976 did he at last leave Juventus of Turin, where he had enjoyed a glorious Indian Summer, for the less demanding Swiss League, and Chiasson. Born in Pircalaba di Sao Paolo, Brazil, on 24 July 1938, he came up through the juniors of the Palmeiras club. As a boy he was nicknamed 'Mazzola' by one of the coaches, owing to his resemblance to the famous Italian footballer, Valentino Mazzola (q.v.). Before the 1958 World Cup in Sweden, he had already been transferred for a large fee to Milan. Feola, the team manager, complained that it had upset his game, that he didn't fit in with the attack. Accordingly he dropped out after the quarter-final, but not before this blond, cheerful, solidly built player had demonstrated his speed, his right-footed shot, his easy skill, his ability in the air, scoring twice in the first game, against Austria. For Milan, where he was now known for the sake of clarity as Altafini, he played seven seasons, making 205 League appearances for 117 goals, no fewer than ninety-two in the first four seasons. Next he spent another seven seasons with Naples in the south, scoring forty-three goals in the first three seasons, a rebuke to Milan, then tailing off with another twenty-eight. Juventus signed him in 1972, and he not only scored nine goals in twenty-three matches in his first season but had a highly effective European Cup, not least with his smoothly taken goals against Derby County in the first-leg semi-final, though perhaps he had his best game of all for them in the quarter-final return at Ujpest. Included at the last moment at the insistence of the President of Juventus, Boniperti, he scored two wonderful opportunist goals to pull the game and the tie out of the fire. His acceleration and leaping remained, for a man of his age, almost miraculous. He proceeded to help Juventus to a couple of Championship wins. He was still a highly effective player for 'Juve', even in his last season, at the age of almost thirty-eight. His Italian origins led to his playing six games for Italy, from 1961, including two in the 1962 Chilean World Cup, while the following year he led Milan's attack at Wembley in the European Cup Final against Benfica, and scored both their goals in a 2–1 victory, using his pace and anticipation to exploit a couple of exquisite through passes by Gianni Rivera (q.v.). Finished his career with Chiasso (Switz.) in 1977.

Amaro Amancio (Spain). Born on 16 October 1939, in the province of Coruna, Amancio joined Deportivo Coruna and was playing Second Division football for them at the age of eighteen. In 1962 Real Madrid took him as an inside-right, converted him into an outside-right with immense success, and in both these positions – winger or striking inside-forward – had magnificent service from him for the next fourteen years. It was not until the end of the 1975–6 season, when he had yet again helped them to win the Championship and had played well in yet another European Cup, that Amancio decided to retire. In 1964, he was probably the best player of the Spanish team which won the Nations Cup, beating Russia in the Final in Madrid; he played on the right wing. In 1966, when Real Madrid at last regained the European Cup, defeating Partizan Belgrade in the Final in Brussels, Amancio was at inside-right, and scored Real's equalizing goal. Strongly and squarely built, very fast, extremely difficult to dispossess with his power allied to close control, Amancio was an exhilarating player to watch. He was sometimes criticized for holding on to the ball too long, but at least he had the capacity and enterprise to take on defenders successfully. In the 1966 World Cup, he was on the right wing again, however, against both Switzerland and West Germany. He won more than forty Spanish caps.

Rodriguez Andrade (Uruguay). This masterly black defender was the nephew of the talented José, Uruguay's right-half when they won the first World Cup in 1930. Twenty years later in Rio, Rodriguez emulated him, playing an heroic game against Brazil in the decisive match. He was just as remarkable in the Swiss World Cup of 1954, though this time he played on the right flank rather than the left; in each case as what we would now call a constructive full-back. Had he not been hurt in the semi-final against Hungary, Uruguay could even have reached the Final. A Penarol of Montevideo player, Andrade was unfailingly cool, not least on the goal line, an impeccable positional player, often creative, in the tradition of the classical Uruguayan wing-half. But his finest game must surely have been that at the Maracana against Brazil in 1950, when his quickness, foresight and last ditch tackling did so much to keep the Brazilians at bay, though he was only twenty. He was also renowned for his good sportsmanship. Even after a game against Brazil in the Atlantic Cup of 1956 when five Uruguayans were sent off, Andrade shook his opponents and the referee by the hand.

Ginacarlo Antognoni (Italy). The great white hope of Italian football after the going of Rivera, Antognoni, blond and well built, is an inside-forward of unusual gifts. He is an excellent and artistic ball player, calm and skilful under pressure, imaginative in his passing, a strong shot. His problem has inevitably been the great pressure put upon such key players in Italian football; he has sometimes been cruelly barracked by Italian fans who preferred their own, local idol to himself. Antognoni was born on 1 April 1954 at Marsciano, Perugia, but surprisingly it was a Fourth (D) Division part-time club, Astimacobi, which persuaded him to turn professional and took him north to Piedmont. He first played League football for them in 1970–71, joined Fiorentina of Florence in 1972 on a half-share basis (a common practice in Italy) and cost them a fortune when they had to pay up the other half. He has, however, been well worth it, playing a consistently large number of Serie A (First Division) games each season, though he does not score many goals. Modest, humorous, occasionally explosive on the field – as we saw when he played against England in 1976 in New York – Antognoni made his debut for Italy against Holland at Rotterdam in the European Nations Cup on 20 November 1974; a difficult baptism, in which he did well.

Luis Artime (Argentina). Some Argentinian players were more concerned with their opponents than the ball during the 1966 World Cup but Artime was certainly not one of them. He proved himself one of the best centre-forwards in the tournament and did credit to the Argentinian tradition of skilful, enterprising ball players, a well-built leader with unusual technique, a formidable change of pace, a fine understanding with his inside-left, Ermindo Onega. Both, strangely enough, had been dropped into the River Plate reserves when Argentina recalled them both for the World Cup. Well served by Onega, Artime raced through to score both goals for Argentina against Spain in a 2–1 win at Villa Park, another goal against Switzerland. Nicknamed 'El Hermoso' ('The Handsome One') goals were very much Artime's game; he scored over 1,000 in a career which took in not only Argentina but Uruguay and Brazil. Born on 2 December 1938, always a thoughtful and conscientious professional, he made his name with the Atlanta club, but in 1962 moved at a huge fee to River Plate. He scored twenty-six goals in twenty-six games in his first season, twenty-four in twenty-three in his second, reviving the fortunes of the club. In 1964 injury limited him to a single game when Argentina won the so-called Little World Cup in Brazil, but the 1966 World Cup was a suitable stage for his talents. That year he left River for Independiente of Buenos Aires. From there he moved on to Nacionale of Montevideo, scoring all their three goals when they won the Intercontinental trophy in 1971 against Panithinaikos; having previously won the South American Copa de Los Libertadores. Next it was Brazil, and Fluminense of Rio, but he voluntarily left them because he found the playing conditions intolerable. The directors had treated him well, but never in a twelve-year career had he known professionals publicly to criticize their colleagues – a reference to the fact that the left winger, Lula, had complained that Artime came out too often to the left wing. Artime was reassuring proof that even in so harsh an epoch, Argentinian football continued to produce gentlemen, as well as thugs. An exemplary footballer.

Gundi Asparoukhov (Bulgaria). The marvellous individual goal that Asparoukhov scored for Bulgaria against England at Wembley in 1968 made up substantially for his disappointing showing in the 1966 World Cup, when he was hampered by an injured ankle. It was his goals which had taken Bulgaria to the World Cup, for on 29 December 1965, when twenty-two, he scored twice for Bulgaria in a play-off match in Florence, thus knocking out the Belgians. His first World Cup game had been an ill-starred match against Hungary in Rancagua in 1962 when Bulgaria lost 6–1, and, alas, by the time Bulgaria played the 1974 World Cup he had died sadly in a motor accident. He remains, however, the best Bulgarian centre-forward there has ever been, a formidable scorer both for Levski, his club, and for the national team, a former basketball player whose jumping to the high ball perhaps owed something to his former sport, a brave, fast player who could shoot with either foot, and had the control to lose the closest of marking.

Ruben Ayala (Argentina). With his abundant moustache, hair hanging down his back, thick thighs and tremendous turn of speed, there is no mistaking Ayala; one of the most dangerous strikers of the day. He established himself in his native Argentina with San Lorenzo de Almagro, materially helped Argentina to qualify for the 1974 World Cup with his five goals in the qualifying tournament, then joined Atletico Madrid, whom he helped to reach the Final of the 1974 European Cup. He himself did not take part in it, having been suspended after his expulsion in the Celtic v Atletico semi-final in Glasgow. A month later he played all six games for Argentina, as a striker, in the West German World Cup, scoring against Haiti. He was then twenty-three. Now more of a midfielder.

Carlos Babington (Argentina). It was a curious transfer which took the blond, curly-haired Babington, an arresting figure of the 1974 World Cup, to Wattenscheid of the West German Second Division, soon afterwards. But Babington, who was sold for £180,000, is used to turns of fortune. An inside-left of many talents, a ball player and a fine passer of the ball, he nearly joined Stoke City on the basis of his English descent, but his father's British passport had lapsed. So he stayed in Argentina, where he began in River Plate's ninth team and made his League debut for Deportivo Colon in 1969, breaking through finally as a member of the Huracan (Buenos Aires) attack. He was added to the Argentinian 1974 World Cup party when they were already on tour, and showed how foolish they had been to think of omitting him with some inspired play, not least against Italy in Stuttgart. He was born on 20 September 1949.

Alan Ball (England). Born in Farnworth, Lancashire, the son of a former Birmingham City inside-forward, Alan Ball senior, who coached him diligently, Alan junior made his debut for England on his twentieth birthday. That was in Belgrade v Yugoslavia in May 1965. The following year he made an outstanding contribution to England's victory in the World Cup, above all in the Final when no one played better and with more stamina than he. Used as a deep outside-right, though his position has really always been inside-forward, he ran the German full-back Schnellinger to exhaustion, forcing the corner which brought the second England goal, taking it himself, and setting up the third for Hurst after a devastating burst down the right and centre. Sixty-five times capped for England and latterly captain, he was once so small that Bolton Wanderers told him 'you'll make a good little jockey' while Wolves rejected him, too. Blackpool had more sense, but they couldn't keep him after the 1966 World Cup, selling him to Everton for over £100,000. He played for England again in the 1970 World Cup in Mexico, a player of great combativity, red-haired, quick, vigorous and shrewd, an excellent user of the short pass, an endless runner. In 1971, Arsenal paid £225,000 to bring him to Highbury, and he continued to play for England until 1975. In 1976, Arsenal sold him to Southampton.

Gordon Banks (England). The one-handed save Banks made from Pelé in the 1970 World Cup at Guadalajara, turning over the bar a point-blank, bouncing header which already had Pelé shouting 'Goal!' was one of the most famous in the story of the game. Not that Banks's approach to goalkeeping was ever sensational or wilfully spectacular; he simply did what he had to do, in the way that it had to be done; sturdy, solid, yet, when occasion demanded it, incomparably agile. In 1966 his fine goalkeeping, not least a couple of memorable saves in the Final against West Germany, helped England to win the World Cup. 'Alf Ramsey's convinced me that my mind's not got to wander,' he said, the day before the game; nor did it. He first played for Chesterfield, where so many famous goalkeepers originated, but in fact he is a Yorkshireman, born in Sheffield. From Saltergate he went to Filbert Street and Leicester City, for whom he played in the Cup Final of 1963. Soon after that, again at Wembley, he won at twenty-four the first of his seventy-three England caps against Brazil, and though Ramsey was displeased he should be beaten by a long range free kick from Pelé ('I'd warned him') he kept his place on the successful European tour that followed. His international career lasted until 1972, by which time he had spent almost five years with his third club, Stoke City, but a motor accident one Sunday morning lost him the sight of an eye and put a premature end to his goalkeeping. He remained with Stoke City as a coach, having established himself as the best goalkeeper of his time. Played in 1977 for Fort Lauderdale, U.S.A.

Frank Barson (England). A centre-half of the old school, attacking kind, Barson was a hard, thoroughly versatile player who won but a single cap for England, in season 1919–20 against Wales, yet is much better remembered than many who won far more; a distinction he shares with another Aston Villa star of the period, Clem Stephenson (q.v.). Curiously enough both were suspended for two weeks by Villa in 1920 for failing to turn up for a League game at Bolton. Both disputed Villa's rule that their players should live in Birmingham; Barson was living in Sheffield. Villa signed him in October 1919 from Barnsley, and he played his first game for them on the 25th against Middlesbrough, away. He was both a dynamic and a dominating player, immensely hard to get past; and sometimes downright hard. Before the 1920 Cup Final at Stamford Bridge, when Villa played Huddersfield, the famous referee J. T. Howcroft came into Villa's dressing-room and warned Barson that 'the first wrong move you make, Barson, off you go!' Small wonder Barson had a subdued first half, but he was at his vigorous best in the second. He could get through the work of two men, and his heading was superb; he was once known to head a goal from thirty yards. Born in the Sheffield steel complex at Grimethorpe, he learned his football in the streets, worshipped Crawshaw of Sheffield Wednesday, was signed by Barnsley when Villa already wanted him, and with fetching modesty opined that he was not good enough for them when Villa finally sought his transfer. He at once inspired a struggling team to win 4–1 at Middlesbrough, saying it was the easiest game he'd ever played in. Disputes with the directors over a dressing-room incident finally led him to move on to Manchester United in 1922. He stayed with them till 1925, helping them to gain promotion, then went on to Watford, Hartlepools, Wigan and Rhyl; with whom he was sent off yet again, now well over forty. He broke his nose four times while playing, and probably took as much as he handed out – once he had to be smuggled away from Everton in a taxi after playing there with Barnsley and infuriating the crowd! But his toughness should not be allowed to obscure the fact that he was a quite exceptional player. In later years he was a trainer with Swansea Town and finally retired to Birmingham.

Billy Bassett (England). In his era the most celebrated of English outside-rights, Bassett's fame was such when he went with the first Football Association touring party to Germany in 1899 that a German defender with a duelling scar followed his every step. When Bassett whimsically strolled behind the goal and back again, Westermarck, the defender, followed him there, too. He won his first FA Cup medal with the club he graced, West Bromwich Albion, in 1888 when he was only eighteen, his first of sixteen international caps the following year. He was very fast, centred with great precision, and, most unusually, was made a director of the club when he retired, in 1905. In 1908, he even became Chairman; an appropriate completion of the career of a player actually born in West Bromwich. Moreover, he was still Chairman over a quarter of a century later.

Cliff Bastin (England). At seventeen, in the summer of 1929, Cliff Bastin joined Arsenal as an inside-left from Exeter City, his local club; a shy Devonian. The following April, at eighteen, now nicknamed 'Boy' Bastin, he helped Arsenal to win the FA Cup against Huddersfield at Wembley, having been most successfully converted into a left winger. The following year, at nineteen, he won the first of his twenty-one England caps. In the summer of 1934 Hugo Meisl, the mentor of the Austrian Wunderteam, assured his brother Willy that if he had Bastin, he would win the World Cup. Bastin's versatility was immense. Very quiet, even withdrawn, but deeply confident of his own abilities, he formed a celebrated partnership for Arsenal with Alex James (q.v.) but he himself if anything preferred running the show at inside-left, where he frequently played for England; and for Arsenal in the 1932 Cup Final, when James was injured. In his early years he had pace, together with a formidable left-footed shot; he set a record with thirty-three goals from the wing in season 1931–2. But he also had a strategy and a highly developed positional sense. He seldom played better than on the England tour of 1933, scoring the equalizer from the wing in Rome against Italy, and doing just as well at inside-left against Switzerland. He made the winning goal for Ted Drake when Arsenal beat Sheffield United in the Cup Final of 1936, and altogether won five League Championship medals with them. From time to time he also played successfully at wing-half. He retired in 1946, and later kept a pub in Exeter.

Carlos Bauer (Brazil). Right-half for Brazil in the 1950

World Cup, left-half in the 1954 tournament, Bauer was an imposing figure in midfield, strong and flexible, versatile and inventive. Born in Sao Paolo of Swiss descent on 21 November 1925. He joined the Sao Paolo club itself as a boy, winning titles with them from youth level up to the professional Championship, but up to the eve of the 1950 World Cup he maintained that his greatest satisfaction was to win the youth title of 1942. In that competition he combined especially well with Brazil's fine inside-right Zizinho (q.v.). The emergence of Brandaozinho as a right-half caused him to move across to the left in Switzerland in 1954, but he will be best remembered for his excellence in the Brazilian team which scored thirteen goals in two matches of the final pool in 1950.

Jim Baxter (Scotland). A left-half back – and on occasion inside-left – with the classical Scottish attributes: absolute command of the ball, a refusal to do things other than in his own time, a sophisticated vision of the game. The tall, dark-haired, elegant Baxter added to all these qualities a matchless left foot, which could be used for passing, picking its way past defenders, or scoring goals. The one he got against England at Wembley in 1963, when he ridiculed the right flank of their defence in a glorious solo, was one of the best seen there since the war. Born in Fife, he joined Rangers from Raith Rovers in 1960 for a mere £7,000, after Burnley had jibbed at £2,500. Five years later, when he had won twenty-nine Scottish caps, they transferred him to Sunderland for over ten times that sum, while he was still only in his mid-twenties. But in 1964, alas, he had broken a leg playing in Vienna in a European Cup tie, and we would never see the same Baxter. Always something of a force of nature, and never the most compulsive trainer, he put on weight and never recaptured the brilliance of those first five years. From Sunderland he moved to Nottingham Forest; but Ibrox saw the exhilarating best of him.

Franz Beckenbauer (West Germany). No player has done more to change the face of football in general and West German football in particular than Franz Beckenbauer, who became the new 'ego ideal' of the German game in the late 1960s, succeeding the more traditional figure of the battling Uwe Seeler (q.v.). Born on 11 September 1945, in Munich, Beckenbauer has now been a star of three World Cups and played in two World Cup Finals, captaining West Germany to success in the second of them. He was captain of the Bayern Munich team which won three European Cups in a row from 1974 to 1976, captain of the West German team which brilliantly won the European Nations Cup of 1972 in Brussels, and was beaten only by the dubious expedient of penalty kicks in the Final of 1976 in Belgrade. Above all, however, he has revolutionized the concept of modern football, with his 'invention' of the attacking sweeper, a role he created and elaborated for his own particular talents with Bayern Munich, and which Helmut Schoen, the team manager, had the courage to try with West Germany after the 1970 World Cup. Tall, dark, curly-headed, with great presence on the field, a consummate technique, a constructive flair equalled by his positional sense in defence, Beckenbauer was a youth international, and played right-half in the excellent West German team which reached the Final of the 1966 World Cup. Perhaps they would have won it had they not used him so cautiously to mark Bobby Charlton. Indeed, it was significant, four years later, that it was precisely the removal of Charlton from the field in Leon, during the World Cup quarter-final, that gave West Germany the initiative when they were behind. Beckenbauer, who scored a somewhat lucky goal, was able to come forward and tip the balance. He has always liked to attack and score goals, with his fine right foot. Indeed, it was one of those typical exciting bursts, in the World Cup semi-final of 1970 in Mexico City against Italy, that led to his being callously chopped down on the edge of the box while in full flight. He was obliged to play out extra time with his arm in a sling; and Italy won 4–3. The Nations Cup Final of 1976 was his hundredth game for West Germany, and a characteristically splendid one. He was criticized for over caution in the 1974 World Cup, and inevitably lost acceleration after his dynamic form of the early 1970s, but he remained a player of unmatched versatility and authority. In April 1977, he shocked the West Germans by accepting a $2,000,000 offer to join New York Cosmos.

Ferenc Bene (Hungary). Small, infinitely incisive forward who made his name at nineteen by his splendid leading of the Hungarian attack when his team won the 1964 Olympic title in Tokyo. Bene scored six against Morocco and rounded off his admirable tournament with a superb individual goal in the Final against Czechoslovakia, running half the length of the field to score. Both fast *and* quick, he was never afraid to go for goal on his own; as he proved again in the 1966 World Cup. Playing now at outside-right, he opened the score at Everton against Brazil with a delightful solo from the wing. First capped when he was barely eighteen, he also functioned successfully as a striking inside-right when Hungary reached the finals of the 1964 Nations Cup, scoring in each game. He also figured in the consistent successes of Ujpest in the Hungarian League during the 1970s, and their fine European Cup runs.

Konstantin Beskov (Russia). Admirable and incisive centre-forward of the Moscow Dynamo team which toured Britain unbeaten in 1945, when he scored freely, and frequently dropped deep behind the attack. In 1952, he played inside-left for Russia in the Helsinki Olympics, a decade later he was manager of their international team. Perhaps the first of the 'modern' centre-forwards. The 1976 Olympiad saw him chief coach to the Russian International team in Montreal.

George Best (Northern Ireland). There are fears that George Best will go down in the history of football as the great lost talent. Not altogether lost. After all, his decade in the British game, with Manchester United and Northern Ireland, was studded with magical goals, astonishing performances. As a forward, there seemed nothing that he could not do. He had the swerve and the acceleration on the wing of a Matthews or a Finney, two splendidly powerful shooting feet, a convulsively quick turn which brought him the decisive goal in the 1968 European Cup Final, a jump which made him immensely dangerous in the air, though he stood only 5 feet 8 inches. He could also, such was his dexterity, flick a coin over his shoulder with his heel so that it landed in his breast pocket.

Born in East Belfast, a strong Protestant area (though he himself is quite unprejudiced) on 22 May 1946, he was discovered by Manchester United's Ulster scout, sent to Old Trafford as a fifteen-year-old with Eric McMordie, another future international, but was so homesick that he went straight back to Belfast. He was persuaded to return, was reconciled to Manchester by a kindly landlady with whom he stayed for years.

A devoted perfectionist who'd made his left foot as good as his right by wearing a gymshoe on the right foot, who'd stayed behind after training with United to kick ball after ball at the crossbar, Best made his League debut against West Bromwich in September 1963. He was seventeen and four months. 'I knew then what I'd always believed,' says Best, 'that I'd find it easy to play in the First Division.' The following April, Northern Ireland capped him for the first time, against Wales.

It was the following season that he and his extraordinary talents truly took wing, but with increasing success came increasing fame, of a kind no previous British footballer had achieved. For Best appealed not only to the football fan but to women: 'If I'd been born ugly,' he once said, 'you'd never have heard of Pelé.' The pressures of publicity were ferocious. He had the celebrity of a pop star, yet had to maintain the fitness of an athlete. As time passed, it all became too much for him, and one does not want to rehearse here the unending dramas, conflicts and scandals, the abrupt retirement from the game followed by almost as abrupt a return, the eventual cancelling by United of his contract. Finally, after a few games in the Fourth Division for Stockport County, he signed a contract in 1976 to play for the Los Angeles Aztecs; and enjoyed both the sunshine and the privacy, returning to England to play for Fulham at £500 a game.

If the most famous game he played was the European Cup Final of 1968, perhaps he was better still in Lisbon, in the same competition against the same team, Benfica, in March 1966. United had been told to 'play it tight', but Best took the battle to Benfica, and destroyed their defence on his own in a wonderful display of skills. Technique, courage, pace, imagination; Best has shown every quality except stability, yet what feats he has performed!

Danny Blanchflower (Northern Ireland). Not only one of the most elegant and accomplished but one of the most fluent professional footballers of the 1950s and early 1960s, Blanchflower was not only a most distinguished captain of Northern Ireland and Spurs, but a writer good enough to be published in the *New Statesman* and the *Observer*. Today, when not playing golf at high stakes and high standards, he writes regularly for the *Sunday Express*; and every word is his own. Born in Belfast, beginning his career with Glentoran, he played for the Irish League, moved to Barnsley in season 1948–9, and found the old-fashioned, football-less training methods most frustrating, though he did win his first cap the following season. Aston Villa signed him early in 1951, and he remained there till he found Villa Park, too, over-conservative and authoritarian for his liking. After weeks of negotiation, Spurs beat their North London rivals Arsenal to his signature for £30,000 in 1954, and he gave them royal service. As a right-half, slim and perceptive, he was neither strong nor fast, but he thought so quickly, his technique was so good, his strategies so shrewd, that he came to dominate any team he played for. Hitting it off perfectly with the former Irish star, now (1958) team manager of Northern Ireland, Peter Doherty (q.v.), he did much to help the team knock Italy out of the World Cup and reach the quarter-finals in Sweden. Before it left, he remarked whimsically that their plan would be 'to equalize before the other team score a goal'. Ireland might have done better still had not Danny's younger brother Jackie, an outstanding, very mobile centre-half, retired from football after the Munich air crash with Manchester United, the previous February. In 1961 Blanchflower captained Spurs to the League and Cup double, in 1962 to the Cup again, in 1963 to the Cupwinners' Cup. That was the season he won the last of his fifty-six caps for Northern Ireland, but in 1976 he was appointed their team manager.

Ernie Blenkinsop (England). 'A bonny full-back; his kicking and volleying were so clean,' said the Scottish winger Alan Morton of this polished left-back. He was transferred from Hull City to his principal club, Sheffield Wednesday, in 1922, and stayed at Hillsborough for twelve years, winning eventually twenty-six caps, sometimes as England's captain, and getting two Championship medals in 1929 and 1930. Born at Cudworth, he relied on skill and anticipation rather than power. 1934 saw him move to Liverpool, but all his caps were won with Sheffield Wednesday.

Oleg Blokhin (Russia). Born in Kiev on 5 November 1952, the son of a mother who was 80-metres hurdles champion of the Ukraine, Blokhin became European Footballer of the Year in 1975, proper recognition for a year in which he had been the salient player of a Dynamo Kiev team which not only won the Cupwinners' Cup but represented Russia *en bloc*. Blond, high-cheekboned, a splendid, well-built athlete who has run 10.8 in the 100 metres – but wants to do better – Blokhin adds to his pace a fine left foot, a flair for getting goals, and deft footwork at speed. He made his name in the Olympic tournament of 1972 in Munich, was a member of the Russian International team eliminated by Chile from the 1974 World Cup, and of the Dynamo Kiev team which that year regained the Russian Championship. A modest young man, Blokhin says that football is his passion rather than his career, that he thinks he could improve in every respect, but above all in his heading. Most clubs and countries would gladly take him as he is; one of the most effective and penetrating forwards in the modern game.

Steve Bloomer (England). Even at this remove, Bloomer's goal-scoring records – he once said that every shot that scored was a good one – are breathtaking. He scored 352 goals in the Football League. For England he got twenty-eight in twenty-three matches, including five against Wales at Cardiff on 16 March 1896. Quick shooting, clever positioning and a flair for the through pass were the chief elements of his game. 'I try to get there first,' he would say, simply. Power had nothing to do with it, for he was a pale, slight figure. He began his career in his habitual and favourite position of inside-right with the Derby Swifts, from whom he moved to Derby County, gaining the first of his England caps in 1895. His debut for Derby County was made in September 1892, and he celebrated by scoring twice for them at Stoke. In 1906 they sold him to Middlesbrough, but he was ecstatically welcomed back to Derby in 1910. He was born at Cradley Heath, was the first pro footballer to be presented with his portrait by the FA when he beat G. O. Smith's record of caps, was interned in Germany where he was coaching throughout the Great War.

Vsevolod Bobrov (Russia). An auburn-haired forward, small but immensely quick and elusive, Bobrov was one of the stars of the Moscow Dynamo team on their unbeaten tour of Britain and Sweden in 1945, a talented ice hockey player whose movements had overtones of that sport. In Britain he played inside-left. In 1952, as an Air Force club player, he led the Russian attack in the Finnish Olympic tournament, when they were knocked out in the first round on a replay by Yugoslavia. It was hardly Bobrov's fault that they lost. In the first, extraordinary game, when Russia came back to draw 5–5 after being 5–1 down with half an hour to play, he scored three of the Russian goals. When Russia lost the replay 3–1, he scored that one, too. With his two colleagues of the 1945 Dynamo tour, he was, by general consent, head and shoulders above the younger Russian players; but Beskov, Trofimov and Bobrov could not shoulder the burden on their own. In 1976, Bobrov was senior coach of the Alma-Ata Kairat club.

Christo Bonev (Bulgaria). Though he fell mysteriously out of favour after the 1974 World Cup, despite being the best player of a disappointing team and scoring against Uruguay, Bonev stands with Kolev and Asparoukhov (q.v.) as the best player his country has yet produced. A tall, well-built, sinuous inside-right with delightful control and great flair, his right foot is formidable, whether he be passing or aiming one of his swerving free kicks at goal. Perhaps it was the fact that he has played for the Lokomotiv Plovdiv club, rather than one of the Sofia teams, which has prevented Bonev gaining the popularity enjoyed by other Bulgarian stars. Born on 3 February 1947, he won his first cap against

West Germany at Hanover in 1967. That Bulgaria qualified at all for the 1974 World Cup was largely thanks to him. His performance against Portugal in Lisbon, when he scored both goals to give Bulgaria a 2–2 draw which virtually qualified them, was devastatingly good.

Rainer Bonhof (West Germany). It was Bonhof who did more than anybody to transform the 1974 West German World Cup team when he came into the side after their defeat by East Germany in Hamburg, Bonhof who burst outside Haan (q.v.) in Munich to lay on the winning goal in the Final. Two years later it was Bonhof who was the most dynamic player of the West German team beaten unluckily on penalties in the finals of the European Nations Cup in Belgrade; and he was still only twenty-four. Born on 29 March 1952, he had made only four appearances for West Germany when the 1974 World Cup began. The Nations Cup Final was his eighteenth, and there were signs he would be the most influential West German player since Franz Beckenbauer. His power, pace, energy and initiative are matched by his astonishing stamina; he is the personification of the modern footballer. He is clearly best suited to an attacking midfield role, that of a right-half, if you wish, though he has also played for his club, Borussia Munchengladbach, and his country, as an overlapping full-back. With Borussia he has won honours in the Bundesliga and the UEFA Cup. There must be many more to come.

Giampiero Boniperti (Italy). The matinée idol of Italian football in the 1940s and 1950s; and one who did not fade. Having retired from the game, loaded with honours, Boniperti, blue-eyed, blond, curly-haired, went on to the board of directors of his only club, Juventus, and eventually became President; the darling of the rich Agnelli family who subsidize it. Above his office desk he hung a photograph of himself in the FIFA line-up against England at Wembley in October 1953; an afternoon when he came in twice from the right wing to score well-taken goals. Four years earlier, at Tottenham, he had filled the same position in an Italian side that had outplayed England, but lost. Born at Barengo, Novara, on 4 July 1928, Boniperti played for the local Momo club, and joined Juventus of Turin as a centre-forward in 1946-7. Progress was very swift. His consummate technique, quickness and opportunism led to his first Italian cap on 9 November 1947. He won another thirty-seven caps, his international career stretching on until 10 December 1960. Fittingly he concluded it, as captain, against Austria, in Naples, though he may have felt it less fitting that Italy should lose, just as they did on his debut against Austria in Vienna. Surprisingly, he scored only eight goals in those thirty-eight games; he was more successful in this respect with Juventus. 'Boni' could play on the right wing, at centre or as a versatile inside-right with equal effect. He did particularly well as inside-right and captain in the trio made up by John Charles and Omar Sivori (q.v.) in the late 1950s and early 1960s.

Jozef Bozsik (Hungary). With Puskas, Kocsis and Hidegkuti (q.v.) Bozsik was one of the great forces of the famous Hungarian team of the early 1950s, conquerors of England at Wembley by 6–3 in November 1953 – an occasion on which Bozsik scored a fulminating goal. His role was that of the attacking, linking right-half, breaking through adventurously from midfield, strong, fast and accomplished. Born on 21 November 1925, winner of 100 caps for Hungary, he won the first of them on 17 August 1947, when Hungary thrashed Bulgaria 9–0. So he was an experienced international by the time he helped Hungary to win the Olympic title of 1952 in Helsinki, a tournament which signalized their emergence from behind the Iron Curtain. Two years later, he was a member of the team so strongly favoured to win the World Cup in Switzerland, but which lost 3–2 to West Germany in the Final in Berne. He was sent off playing against Brazil, also in Berne. Four years later, a slowing veteran by now, he was inexplicably and unsuccessfully used in the Hidegkuti position of deep centre-forward in the Swedish World Cup. When Puskas, Kocsis and Czibor 'defected' from the Honved team on tour in 1956, Bozsik had gone back to Hungary. He was a Member of the House of Deputies and in the 1970s briefly became manager of the national team, but gave up after a heart attack.

Paul Breitner (West Germany). Tall, long-legged, bushy-haired, an avowed Maoist who adopted a Vietnam orphan but lives an opulent life in Spain, Breitner's ambition is to retire early from football and found a school for handicapped children. Meanwhile he has been one of the most spectacular and controversial players of his day, a star of the West German team which won the 1972 Nations Cup in Brussels, the 1974 World Cup in Munich. He then insisted on leaving the club with which he had grown up, Bayern Munich, and was sold at a huge sum to Real Madrid, where he instantly switched with success from attacking full-back to midfield. Breitner is very much in the mould of the Total Footballer, fast, versatile, a goal scorer as well as a defender. In the 1974 World Cup his goal scoring was of vital consequence. He broke the deadlock against Chile in Berlin with a tremendous shot from outside the box, got the first goal against Yugoslavia in Dusseldorf, and a penalty in the Final to equalize against Holland. It was typical of him that he should be ready to take it, under such pressure; but then reticence and uncertainty are not among Breitner's problems. Born in Bavaria on 5 September 1951, he became an international figure as the twenty-year-old attacking left-back of the West German Nations Cup team of 1972, playing wonderfully well against England in the quarter-final at Wembley. His left-wing politics made him a fish out of water at Bayern, where the tendency, embodied by Beckenbauer (q.v.), was further to the right, and his departure was not altogether surprising. He has had his vicissitudes. A missile hurled by a spectator broke his leg in Atvidaberg, Sweden, in 1973, but he had recovered in time to help Bayern win their first European Cup in May 1974 in Brussels. After the World Cup Final, he at first announced he would not play for Germany again, changed his mind, apologized, but again said he would not play, early in 1976. In season 1977–8, he returned to West Germany to play for Brunswick.

Billy Bremner (Scotland). A tiny, red-haired midfield player of disproportionate influence and energy, Bremner was the inspiration of Scotland in the 1974 World Cup, just as for so many years he had been the inspiration of Leeds United, winning League, Cup and Fairs Cup medals with them. Born in Stirling on 9 December 1942, he came to Leeds as a schoolboy international outside-right from Gowanhill Juniors, and made his League debut in January 1960, at the age of seventeen. It's said that he shared a room with Don Revie, England's future manager, then still a Leeds player, who persuaded him to kneel and pray. The prayers appear to have been answered since Bremner, becoming by turns an inside-right then a right-half, metamorphosed into one of the most effective players of his day, although he did not grow above 5 feet $5\frac{1}{2}$ inches. A fierce, sometimes an over-fierce, competitor, he had almost every gift; he was exceedingly quick, skilful on the ball, a strong tackler, a good distributor, with a remarkably strong right-footed shot. Moreover, though he was never one for monastic life, he was fit enough still to be a major force in his mid-thirties; and this despite the huge number of games he had played. The first of his many Scottish caps was won against England at Hampden

Park in April 1966. His international career concluded unhappily in 1975, after incidents while Scotland were visiting Copenhagen for a Nations Cup match against Denmark. After he had played so often and so well for Scotland, it was sad that Bremner's departure from the team should be such a brusque anticlimax. In 1976, he left Leeds to captain Hull City.

Charlie Buchan (England). The Great War bisected the career of this famous inside-forward, renowned for a wayward brilliance which condemned him to making only a handful of appearances for England; he was allegedly 'too clever' for those around him.

Certainly he wasn't 'too clever' for the famous Sunderland attack of the years just before 1914, when Buchan, tall, long-legged, enormously adroit, was the inside-right, superbly complemented by the equally large and gifted George Holley.

Buchan was the son of Aberdonian parents, born and brought up in South East London. Woolwich Arsenal, as they were till 1913 and their move to Highbury, had him as an amateur, but they quarrelled with him over eleven shillings expenses, and he moved to Leyton, then Sunderland. By the time Arsenal wanted him back it was 1925, and they had to pay Sunderland a lump sum and £100 a goal; a unique bargain and a good one for Arsenal, since Buchan promptly invented the Third Back (stopper centre-half) game and skippered them into the 1927 Cup Final. He retired the following year to become a successful journalist and broadcaster.

Ronnie Burgess (Wales). An attacking left-half who loved to go forward; even, at times, to excess. Burgess, a lean, wiry player not improperly compared with a greyhound, learned his football on the South Wales slagheaps. Spurs first turned him down, then, luckily for them, changed their mind and signed him, as a right-half, before the war from the little Cwm Villa club. He gained a regular place in the Welsh international team at left-half during the war, and held it till 1954, the year he left Tottenham to become a successful player-coach with Swansea Town. He was a prominent member of the Tottenham team which won the Second Division Championship in 1950, the First in 1951. Born at Cwm, he became manager of Watford in later years.

Johnny Carey (Ireland). 'Keep on playing football,' Johnny Carey instructed his Manchester United team when they fell behind to Blackpool in the 1948 Cup Final. They did, and they won. Carey himself always believed in the purist's approach. A Dubliner, he joined Manchester United from the local St James's Gate club for a paltry £200 in November 1936 as an inside-forward, became a wing-half after the war, during which he served with the Army in Italy, and finally, with great success, a highly constructive and infallibly cool right-back, strong in the tackle and a good distributor. He was at right-half when he captained the Rest of Europe against Britain in Glasgow in May 1947. Twenty-five times capped for Eire and a regular choice for the combined Ireland team till it ceased to exist, alas, in 1949. Subsequently he became manager of Blackburn Rovers, Everton, Leyton Orient and Nottingham Forest.

Raich Carter (England). A masterly inside-forward whose career spanned the Second World War. Durham born, a schoolboy soccer international and a good swimmer, he almost eluded Sunderland, his local club, for Leicester City had him as an amateur, but inexplicably let him go back to the North East, and Sunderland, in 1931. There he stayed for fourteen years, a major figure in their successive Cup (1936) and League (1937) triumphs. First capped for England in 1934, winning thirteen caps in all, he was slow to establish himself. It was nine full years later that he came into the brilliant wartime England forward-line as an ideal partner to Matthews (q.v.). A deft ball player, a splendid shot with either foot, a superb passer of the ball, he joined Derby County in 1945, establishing a memorable partnership with Peter Doherty (q.v.) which brought the Cup victory – Derby's first major honour – in 1946. Carter went on to become a formidable player-manager of Hull, silver-haired and peremptory, guiding them out of the Third Division (North). His real name is Horatio; he would subsequently manage Leeds United.

Mike Channon (England). Born at Orcheston, a Wiltshireman standing over 6 feet and weighing over 12 stone, Mike Channon is one of the most rhythmic and rapid movers in British football, as thoroughbred in style as the horses he rears on his farm. Making his first appearance for Southampton as a teenager in season 1965–6, he celebrated ten distinguished years of service by helping them to win the FA Cup against Manchester United in May 1976. Then he went on England's tour of the United States and played superbly, above all against Italy in New York when he was captain for the day, and celebrated with two rocketing goals. His great acceleration, the power of his right-footed shot, were very much in evidence. When he played the third match of the tour against Team America in Philadelphia, it was his thirty-first international game. The first was a most successful appearance against Yugoslavia at Wembley in October 1972; after which he was promptly and mysteriously dropped. So he was again, disastrously, for the World Cup qualifying match against Poland in Katowice the following year. But he was back in the team again, most successfully, for the next game, when Russia were beaten in Moscow, and there he stayed. Though he feels he can 'hit the line from both sides', he is certainly at his best on the right. Joined Manchester City in summer 1977.

John Charles (Wales). One of the best of all Welsh footballers, a mighty centre-half who became a formidable centre-forward, and spent his most successful years playing for Juventus of Turin in the Italian League. Born in Swansea on 12 December 1931, Leeds United took him at fifteen to Elland Road, and by early 1949 he was their precocious seventeen-year-old centre-half, good enough to win a first cap for Wales; though he had a disappointing game. Massively built, unrivalled in the air, possessed of a great burst of speed and technique unusual in one so large, Charles really found himself when Leeds converted him to centre-forward. He got 150 goals for them, including a record forty-two in the Second Division in 1953–4. In the summer of 1957 Juventus paid £65,000 for his transfer, and he helped them to win three out of the next four Championships, becoming the idol of Turin, nicknamed 'King John'. Thirty-eight times capped for Wales, he returned briefly to Leeds in 1962, but joined Roma the following November. Both he and his brother Mel played for Wales in the 1958 World Cup.

Bobby Charlton (England). After Stanley Matthews (q.v.) no English player made the same impact abroad as Bobby Charlton, hailed in South America, lauded in Russia, eulogized in Italy. If anything his reputation was higher in Europe than it was in Britain. Born in Ashington, County Northumberland, in 1938, his brother Jackie an accomplished centre-half, his cousins the Milburns a famous family of League footballers, he joined Manchester United at fifteen, turned professional at seventeen, and made his League debut as a centre-forward in October 1956, scoring twice. In 1957 he was at inside-left in the Cup Final, lost against Aston Villa. In February 1958, he survived the disastrous

Munich air crash when so many United players perished. It left deep psychological wounds which took a very long time to heal. Always shy and detached, Charlton became all the more introverted. True, his career continued to thrive. His brilliant play, his glorious left-footed shooting, helped Manchester United to reach the 1958 Cup Final, too; although they lost again, this time to Bolton. At Hampden Park, he made his international debut against Scotland. But when England lost 5–0 to Yugoslavia in May in Belgrade – the city where United had played immediately before the crash – Charlton was brusquely and debatably dropped. He did not get a single game in the 1958 World Cup, although England's forwards looked so weary and inept throughout. By 1962, however, he had become an outside-left, his beautiful swerve outside the back, his pace, his shooting – with left foot now as well as right – making him infinitely dangerous. In the Chilean World Cup, he had an especially good game, and scored a fine goal, against Argentina in Rancagua. Now honours showered upon him. By the 1966 World Cup, he had been converted into a deep-lying centre-forward, his blond hair thinning now, using the long cross-field pass with enthusiasm, and using his skill in beating a man, his stupendous shot, to score a glorious long range right-foot goal against Mexico, two in the semi-final against Portugal. He was duly voted European Footballer of the Year for 1966. In 1968, he helped Manchester United become the first English team ever to win the European Cup, when his blond head – even thinner on top by now – actually and unusually scored a goal. In 1970, he was again a World Cup player, showing such authority that it still seems likely that England would have kept their lead against West Germany in the quarter-final at Leon, had he not been contentiously substituted. That brought his total to 106 caps, beating the record set by Billy Wright (q.v.). On retirement he became manager of Preston North End, but resigned on a point of principle in 1975–6 and joined a travel agency. His forty-nine goals for England still stand as a formidable record, while he and Jackie share with the brothers Walter of West Germany the distinction of both appearing in a World Cup winning side.

Zlatko Cjaicowski (Yugoslavia). Now a small, plump manager working in West Germany, where he has had charge of such clubs as Bayern Munich and Cologne, Cjaicowski, a most resilient and authoritative right-half, captained Yugoslavia both in the 1950 and the 1954 World Cups. Blond and short, he was, however, both powerful and technically accomplished. He played for Partizan of Belgrade, he was capped fifty-five times for his country, and he was in the FIFA team which held England to a draw at Wembley in October 1953. His brother played for Yugoslavia on the left wing in the 1950 World Cup.

Ray Clemence (Liverpool). Recognized now as one of the world's best goalkeepers, Clemence did not have an easy rise to fame. Born in Skegness, a commanding six-footer, weighing twelve stone, he was actually working as a deckchair attendant on the beach when Scunthorpe offered him a chance. So well did he do with the Lincolnshire club that Liverpool signed him, but he had to wait some time in the shadows, despite gaining Under 23 English honours, as deputy to Tommy Lawrence, before he at last gained a regular place in the Liverpool team. Since then he has helped them to win Cup, League and UEFA Cup – twice. He is a supple and shrewd goalkeeper, gymnastic enough to reach difficult shots, prehensile enough to grasp them in full flight. England capped him in their two World Cup qualifying matches against Wales in 1973, but it was not till May 1974 that he at last displaced his gifted rival Peter Shilton in the England goal, and had a long run of games. If it is true that he let Scotland's winning goal through his legs at Hampden in May 1976, it is equally true that he went on to play majestically on the American tour, and against Finland in the World Cup in Helsinki, not to mention the 1977 European Cup Final, in Rome.

Mario Coluna (Portugal). Initially an inside-left, latterly a left-half, scorer of a staggering, long range, left-footed goal both in the European Cup Final of 1961 and that of 1962, Coluna was Portugal's captain in the 1966 World Cup. Three years earlier, on the Wembley ground where they lost the semi-final to England, his injury, when fouled by Pivatelli, was probably the chief reason why Benfica relinquished their European Cup to Milan. A black, lean, splendidly made athlete from Lourenço Marques in Mozambique, where he was born on 6 August 1935, his initial interest was in fact athletics, and he set the Mozambique long jump record. Deportivo, the local club, actually transferred him to Benfica as an inside-forward, and he subsequently played outside-left before settling down at inside-forward. When he left Benfica, it was to play briefly in France for Lyon.

Rik Coppens (Belgium). Known as the centre-forward who played with his back to the goal, the chunkily built Coppens was chief rival to Mermans (q.v.) as the best Belgian leader of his time. Born in 1930, the son of a wealthy fish merchant, he was thus always able to resist the many offers he had to play abroad, and spent his career with his local club in Beerschot. Coppens kept the ball on the ground, where he was at his strongest. He led the Belgian attack against England and Italy in the 1954 World Cup in Switzerland, and scored against England. He was something of an *enfant terrible* in Belgian football, controversial and unfailingly outspoken.

Warney Cresswell (England). A blond full-back, ahead of his time in his penchant for attack. He was a right-back when in the season 1921–2 Sunderland paid nearby South Shields what was then a record £5,500 for his transfer; he had already won the first two of his ten England caps. An elegant player, never in a hurry, he moved again in 1926 when Everton signed him, and was at left-back in their Championship winning team of 1927–8.

Bob Crompton (England). Forty-two times capped for England at a time when international matches were relatively few, Bob Crompton was the most illustrious right-back of his era, a pillar of the Blackburn Rovers club, and one half of the famous Crompton–Jesse Pennington full-back partnership for England. Born in Blackburn, he played for them from 1896 to 1920, a large, calm, physically robust defender, praised by Charlie Buchan (q.v.) as 'the best kicker of a ball I ever ran across'. His positioning was sound, his authority great, and he served Rovers for forty years, as player, honorary manager, director and advisor. He was born in 1879, played for the successful Moss Street Board School team, became an apprentice plumber when he left school, and was found by Rovers playing in Sunday School football. He was so keen to continue as an amateur swimmer and water polo player that he would not play as a professional for Blackburn for two full seasons. He was a centre-half then, and had his first chance in the League team there at the end of season 1896–7, without much success. At the start of the following season, however, Glover, the regular right-back, was injured, and Crompton came in to partner the well-known Tom Brandon, whose fame he was destined to surpass. He stood 5 feet $9\frac{1}{2}$ inches, he weighed $12\frac{1}{2}$ stone, and it is interesting that despite his reputation for rugged play, a contemporary account should insist that 'his nature and training are all against this style ... indeed it is a frequent cause of complaint with the fiercer section of the club's supporters that he does not use his weight against opponents more frequently'. The account went on, 'Perhaps he balloons the ball rather too much for the perfect back' but conceded 'it takes a very strong charge indeed to knock him off his quarry'. He was not fast, and the story was told of him that in an Inter-League match against the Scots at Newcastle, he surprised everybody by keeping pace with the fleet Alec Smith of Rangers. After the game, he admitted 'he had hold of the latter's breeches!'

Sammy Crooks (England). If Stanley Matthews (q.v.) emerged as the most remarkable English outside-right between the wars, Sammy Crooks was one of the most effective, twenty-six times capped between 1930 and 1937, often to the exclusion of Matthews himself. He was a very different type of player, small and fast and very direct, making up with Duncan (q.v.) a famous pair of wingers for Derby County. Yet another North Easterner, he was born at Bear Par, County Durham, worked in a colliery, had a short spell with the colliery team, Brandon Juniors and Tow Law, then turned professional as an inside-forward with Durham City. His lack of height led them to put him on the right wing, with instant success, and Derby County bought him in 1927. He played 400 games for them, and was even a candidate for their 1946 Cup winning team, though the place eventually went to Harrison. But Crooks was still fit enough to appear for Derby in 1946–7, the season in which League football was resumed.

Johan Cruyff (Holland). With the waning of Pelé, Cruyff became by general consent the outstanding footballer of the 1970s, challenged perhaps only by Franz Beckenbauer. He was certainly the richest and the most expensive. When Barcelona persuaded Ajax of Amsterdam to part with him in the autumn of 1974, the combined transfer and personal contract came to some £880,000, for two years, and when after stormy goings-on in the spring Barcelona decided to keep him, it cost them 48 million pesetas (£400,000) for a single year. Meanwhile, in the Finals of the European Nations Cup in Zagreb Cruyff, whose dazzling play against Belgium had won Holland the quarter-finals, added no lustre to his fame, being embroiled in controversy both on and off the field; not for the first time. Of his immense talent, however, there can be no doubt; a slender, wiry, galvanically quick and mobile centre-forward with superb control, a beautiful touch, wonderful reflexes, unusual constructive powers. The almost incredible rapidity of his exchange with Johan Neeskens (q.v.) which brought Holland their first goal in the World Cup final pool against Brazil at Dortmund in June 1974 was matched by the goal he swept in himself from Krol's cross; two almost matchless pieces of virtuosity. Cruyff has denied he is especially fast, saying that it is merely a question of getting off the mark quicker; perhaps a distinction without a difference. His father died when he was small, his mother once scrubbed the floors of the Ajax club, through whose junior teams he graduated. Born on 25 April 1947, he much admired the lanky Faas Wilkes (q.v.), Holland's best player of the time. His debut for Holland, against Czechoslovakia, was ill augured; he retaliated to a foul and was banned from the team for a year, the start of a tempestuous but brilliant international career. It was a long time before he and his club colleagues made Holland a team as formidable as Ajax, who won three European Cups in a row between 1971 and 1973. When Cruyff left, following his mentor Rinus Michels to Barcelona (Michels returned there in 1976), Ajax fell apart. Cruyff meanwhile was European Footballer of the Year no fewer than three times between 1971 and 1974. This though the World Cup Final was an anticlimax for him and for Holland. Brought down by Hoeness (q.v.) in the very first minute, Cruyff gained a penalty from which Neeskens gave Holland the lead; but they failed to consolidate their advantage. To his string of Championships with Ajax, he added another with Barcelona in 1974–5, transforming the team as soon as he was given clearance to play, and taking them at a rate of knots from the depths to the top of the table. Among his other accomplishments is that of being an excellent natural linguist, conversant with Spanish, English, French, German and Italian.

Teofilo Cubillas (Peru). He was only twenty when he played so dashingly for Peru as a striking inside-forward in the 1970 World Cup, a coloured player of great speed, unusual ball skills, and initiative. In the opening game, against Bulgaria in Leon, he scored the winning goal with a strong, right-footed shot after a dazzling solo. A deflected free kick brought him another goal against West Germany, and he added two more against Morocco. This took Peru through to the quarter-finals, but although Brazil beat them at Guadalajara, it was Cubillas who scored their second goal. Developed by the Alianza club of Lima, he was transferred after the tournament to the Swiss club, Basel, and later to Porto, of Portugal, where he continued to score spectacular goals.

Stanley Cullis (England). Born at Ellesmere Port, Cheshire, of Black Country parents, it was perhaps inevitable that Cullis should sign for Wolverhampton Wanderers, with whom he spent the whole of his splendid career, retiring at the early age of thirty-one in 1947 to become a most successful manager, wedded to teams which deployed wingers and the long ball. In May 1939, in Bucharest he had become the then youngest captain of England when he led the team against Rumania, at the age of twenty-two. Cullis was a centre-half who would have fitted admirably and eagerly into the pattern of Total Football, for he loved to attack, and he had the ball control to do it. His physical power, firm tackling, fine heading made him a thoroughly competent third back, too. He was captain of Wolves when they so surprisingly were thrashed by Portsmouth in the 1939 Final, losing the League, too; as they did once more in the heatwave of 1947, again under his captaincy. On leaving Wolves in 1964, he became for several years manager of Birmingham City, but times and styles had changed and he was unable to repeat his successes of the 1950s. He won a dozen full caps, but perhaps reached his international peak in the war when he made up a superlative half-back line for England with Cliff Britton and Joe Mercer, with whom he also represented the Army. His curious, arms akimbo, style earned him the nickname of 'Flipper'.

Zoltan Czibor (Hungary). A lively, rapid, incisive outside-left who was a splendid foil to Puskas, Kocsis and Hidegkuti (q.v.) in the Hungarian team of the 1950s, of which he was a member when they won the Olympic title at Helsinki in 1952, and lost the World Cup Final in Berne in 1954. Born in Budapest in 1929, only 5 feet 7 inches tall, he went to Honved, the Army club, from Ferencvaros, and there struck up a famous partnership with Puskas. When Puskas was injured during the 1954 World Cup, Czibor showed his versatility by moving into the inside-left position, where he played with great flair and success. His performance against Brazil, in the quarter-finals, and Uruguay, in the semi-finals, was perhaps decisive. He scored the first goal against Uruguay and, put back on the wing when Puskas controversially returned for the Final, scored against Germany then. After the 1956 Revolution he stayed outside Hungary with other members of the Honved team, tried unsuccessfully to join Roma but with Kocsis (q.v.) was taken on in Spain by Barcelona; having by then won forty-three Hungarian international caps. He was as lively as ever in the Barcelona team, which reached the Final of the European Cup against Benfica in Berne in May 1961, and he scored Barcelona's first goal.

Julien Da Rui (France). Julien Da Rui was the only Frenchman in the Rest of Europe team beaten 6–1 at Hampden Park by Great Britain in May 1947; the same season in which his brave and acrobatic goalkeeping had helped Roubaix-Tourcoing to win the French Championship. Da Rui played twenty-five times for France, winning his first international cap on 16 March 1939, against Hungary, in Paris, his last on 17 October 1948, again in Paris, against Belgium.

Dixie Dean (England). Actually he hated to be called Dixie; his name was Bill. Powerfully built, a phenomenal header of a ball, he set up in 1927–8 a First Division scoring record of sixty goals which will surely never be beaten; the last three coming against Arsenal at Goodison Park in the final match of the season.

Born in Birkenhead, Dean, a dark, muscular man, began his career with local Tranmere Rovers, then made the short trip across the Mersey to Everton with whom his halcyon years were spent. He won Championship medals with them in 1928 and 1932, a Cup medal in 1933, scoring one of his club's three goals against Manchester City. He also played sixteen times for England. Concluding his career with Notts County, he brought his total of League goals to the formidable number of 379.

Kazimierz Deyna (Poland). An inside-right of classical gifts – call him midfield player if you must – nothing became Deyna like the leaving of . . . Lubanski. When that brilliant forward was hurt playing for Poland against England in Katowice in 1973, Deyna emerged from beneath his shadow to become the dominant player of a splendid team. Then twenty-six, he had already scored both Poland's goals when they won the Olympic Final the previous year. Now with his graceful control, his impeccable passing, his readiness to close in on goal for a shot, he helped them qualify for the 1974 World Cup Finals, and surpass themselves when they reached West Germany. Born near Danzig at Starogard Gdanski, he established himself, however, in the capital with Legia Warsaw. The World Cup over, he yearned to play abroad, even threatened to retire in 1975. Polish stars, after all, earn relatively little.

Alfredo Di Stefano (Argentina and Spain). Di Stefano was playing Total Football before anyone had heard of it. His immense versatility and phenomenal stamina, built up by road running in Buenos Aires, enabled him to become that rarity even in the Total Football of today; a forward who could actually defend. Moreover his lung power seemed at times to enable him to take a shot at goal one minute, make a saving slide tackle in his own penalty area the next. He was the guiding genius of the Real Madrid teams which won the first five European Cups in a row between 1956 and 1960. Born in July 1926 in Buenos Aires, the son of an immigrant from Capri who was also a footballer, Di Stefano played for River Plate, won seven caps for his country, then was lured in 1949 to Bogota, Colombia, to play at a vast salary for the Millionarios club. There he stayed till 1953, when Real and Barcelona both claimed to have signed him; a judgement of Solomon by the Spanish FA said they should share him, but Barcelona waived their claims after he had begun with Real. Lucky Real! They had more than a decade of brilliant service; he played for the Rest of the World against England in 1963, was still Real's leader in the European Cup Final of 1962. Blond, well built, with every possible gift – pace, imagination, faultless control, balance, shooting power, heading ability – he dominated the European game, and Real with him, scoring forty-nine in European cup-ties. He was less successful when he played thirty-one times for Spain, and sat out the World Cup in Chile in 1962 with an injury. Later he managed Boca Juniors, Valencia and other clubs.

Didì (Brazil). One of the finest of all Brazilian players, the peerless, creative inside-forward ideally suited to the 4–2–4 formation with which Brazil won the 1958 World Cup. Dark, lean and intense, his face like an African tribal mask, Didì had already played in the 1954 World Cup in Switzerland, a splendid technician and a magnificent passer of a ball, celebrated too for his 'falling leaf' free kicks, one of which brought the goal which beat Peru in Rio to qualify Brazil for the World Cup Finals. By an irony, Didì twelve years later was manager of the Peruvian national team which got to the Finals in Mexico and was actually knocked out by Brazil in the quarter-final round. Meanwhile, in 1962, he had helped Brazil, in Chile, to win another World Cup. Born in Campos, he went to Rio to play for Madureiro Fluminense, then Botafogo, spent a bitter season of frustration with Real Madrid in 1959–60 – Di Stefano just would not accept him – but returned to Botafogo, and fresh triumphs.

Jimmy Dimmock (England). An outside-left, London born, whose solo run and left-foot shot gave Tottenham Hotspur the FA Cup Final of 1921 against Wolves. Dimmock was capped only three times for England but his skill was such that it's said the great Irish back Bill McCracken once walked off the field in despair at ever tackling him. Charles Buchan called him 'in his day the finest individualist in the game'.

Peter Doherty (Northern Ireland). A wiry, red-haired inside-left who would have fitted perfectly into the Total Football of today, such was his versatility and stamina. Coleraine, his local club, snubbed him, so he joined Glentoran instead, moving to England, and Blackpool, in 1933 for £3,000. The fee was £10,000 by the time he joined Manchester City three years later, gaining a Championship medal in 1937. During the war he played, first as a guest, for Derby County. His notable partnership with Raich Carter enabled them to win the Cup Final of 1946.

But Doherty, never afraid to speak his mind at a time when professional footballers were much more subdued than today, seldom stayed long at any club. He moved to Huddersfield Town, became player–manager of Doncaster Rovers, and all this time was a gallant performer for all-Ireland; as they were till 1949. Later he became manager of Bristol City and the first team manager of his beloved Northern Ireland, whom he guided to the Finals of the 1958 World Cup at the expense of mighty Italy. As a player, his swerve, his pace, his energy, his perception, his fine left foot, his courage in the goalmouth made him one of the leading inside-forwards of his day.

Dally Duncan (Scotland). One of the most effective left-wingers between the wars, Duncan won nine home international caps for Scotland and scored both goals when England were beaten 2–0 at Hampden Park in April 1935. His nickname had nothing to do with his pace, which till his veteran years (he won a Cup medal with Derby as late as 1946) was considerable. It derived from the fact that as a little boy out on a walk, he'd hang behind to kick stones. Hull City were his first English club (1929), but it was with Derby (1932) that he made his name, forming a dashing pair of wingers with Sammy Crooks (q.v.). On retirement he became manager of Luton Town, then Blackburn Rovers; a small, dark man with very good close control, and an exceptional left foot. An Aberdonian who never played for Aberdeen, his junior club was called Aberdeen Violet. There he was found by Hull, whom he helped to reach the semi-final of the Cup in 1930, when they drew with the then resplendent Arsenal.

Dragan Dzajic (Yugoslavia). A goal in each of Yugoslavia's games in the Finals of the European Nations Cup of June 1976 was Dzajic's substantial answer to those who said his international career was finished. The second goal, scored directly from a beautifully struck, inevitably left-footed, free kick in the Third Place match against Holland in Zagreb was a memorable one. Eight years earlier, in the same competition, played in Italy, he had scored a beautifully taken winner against England in the semi-final, and another against Italy in the Final. Born on 30 May 1946, in Belgrade, he spent many years with the Red Star club, for whom he made his debut on 4 June 1963, taking as his mentor and hero Josip Skoblar, another fine left-winger. But Dzajic has always been his own man, a superb winger at a time when wingers were going out of fashion; and still there when they returned. He helped Yugoslavia win through to the World Cup Finals of 1974, though he himself had a rather disappointing tournament in West Germany. In 1975, allowed to play abroad at last, he unexpectedly joined the French League club Bastia, of Corsica; a little club, he said, but one where he was happy. Returned to Red Star in 1977.

Ralf Edstroem (Sweden). Tall, willowy, standing well over 6 feet, a formidable header of the ball with a delicate touch on the ground, Edstroem will never score a finer goal than he did in the Finals of the 1974 World Cup with a searing volley in Dusseldorf, against West Germany. Born on 7 October 1952, he became a star in Europe in August 1972, when he scored all three of Sweden's goals against Russia in Gothenburg. The previous year he had left his original club, Degerfors, for Atvidaberg, for whom he proceeded to score sixteen goals. His excellent foil and partner Sandberg scored as many, helping Atvidaberg to win the Championship; their partnership was equally effective in the 1974 World Cup. By that time, however, both were with foreign clubs, Sandberg with Kaiserslautern in West Germany, while Edstroem had joined PSV Eindhoven in the summer of 1973, helping them to win League titles in Holland in 1975 and 1976. A pleasant, modest, fluent young man, Edstroem's composed temperament fits him ideally for important matches. Returned to Sweden in 1977.

Duncan Edwards (England). Will always be mourned as one of the great, lost talents of English football. He was only twenty-one when he was fatally injured in the Munich air crash of February 1958, when an Elizabethan aircraft carrying the Manchester United team back from a European Cup tie in Belgrade crashed in the snow. Edwards lingered pitifully on for a few days, thanks to his own great strength and an artificial kidney machine, but finally succumbed. A left-half of outstanding physique, great drive and an extraordinary left-footed shot, he had already been a Manchester United first teamer since he was seventeen, had made his representative debut at Bologna in 1954 in the first ever Under 23 international, and had gone on to play no fewer than eighteen times for England, scoring a decisive goal against West Germany in Berlin in May 1956. A Midlander from Dudley, Staffs, Manchester United's well-known powers of prevailing in the case of coveted young footballers brought him to Old Trafford when geography suggested he might stay in the Midlands. He might well have been a star of three or four World Cups; but what use is speculation?

Willis Edwards (England). Thought by many experts to have been the outstanding English right-half between the wars, Edwards won seventeen England caps between 1925 and 1930, the equivalent of many more today. 'A really grand all round player,' said the illustrious Scottish outside-left, Alan Morton, of him. 'So firm on the ball, yet so light in his feet and accurate in his passing.' Born in Newton, Derbyshire, he began with local Chesterfield, joined Leeds United in 1925 for £1,500, and played for them right through to 1939, making 450 League appearances.

Eusebio (Portugal). Probably the best Portuguese international forward of all time, a major figure of the 1966 World Cup, in which he finished leading scorer with nine goals, Eusebio Ferreira Da Silva came to Lisbon from his native Lourenço Marques as a nineteen-year-old in 1961 and succeeded instantly. Bought by Benfica for a mere £7,500, he was quickly put into the Paris Tournament to play against Santos and Pelé, scoring three goals. A few months later he was flown out to Montevideo to play against Penarol in the Intercontinental Cup and distinguished himself again, with a fine goal. The following year his devastating right-footed shooting decided the European Cup Final in Amsterdam in Benfica's favour against Real Madrid – he scored twice – and Puskas, who had scored three, conferred on him the accolade by presenting him with his jersey at the end of the game. The following year when the European Cup Final was played at Wembley, Eusebio scored again, versus Milan, but it was not enough to save Benfica from defeat. His beautifully loose, flowing movement, his tremendous acceleration, his fine control, his explosive right foot, made him second only to Pelé among the world's forwards of his time. Knee injuries subverted his form in the 1970s, when he played for such clubs as Boston (Mass.) and Mexico's Monterey, but he had in the meantime played a glorious 1966 World Cup, his volley of superb goals sinking the North Koreans in the semi-finals at Everton, after they'd established a 3–0 lead in the quarter-finals after only twenty minutes.

Giacinto Facchetti (Italy). It was a pity Facchetti should lose his temper when his equalizing goal was properly disallowed at the end of Italy's match with England in New York in May 1976, flailing in turn at the two English full-backs. As his defenders said, it wasn't typical. Indeed, he had sometimes been criticized during his long career precisely for his restraint. A left-back standing well over 6 feet with a tremendous right-footed shot and a penchant for scoring goals, Italy had turned him into a sweeper after their disastrous World Cup of 1974. It was Facchetti's third. He had been disappointed with himself in England in 1966, but did better in Mexico, where he helped Italy to reach the 1970 Final. Born on 18 July 1942 at Treviglio, Bergamo, and once a centre-forward, he joined Internazionale of Milan as a youth, making his debut for them in Rome in May 1961, playing his first game for Italy against Turkey in Istanbul on 27 March 1963. He went on to establish a record number of caps, of which he now has over eighty. With Inter, he won several Italian Championships, two European Cups, two Intercontinental titles.

Elias Figueroa (Chile). One of the best centre-halves in the 1974 World Cup, though he very nearly missed it. Chile had to go to great lengths to have him finally released by his Brazilian club, Internacional of Porto Alegre. It would have been ironic as well as sad had the tall, resilient Figueroa missed a tournament which he had done so much to help Chile reach. He had been especially dominant when they drew 0–0 against Russia in Moscow, having already won their South American group, and being obliged to play-off. In 1970, in fact, Figueroa had not been able to play for Chile in the World Cup eliminating series, being refused permission by Penarol of Montevideo, the club for whom he was then playing. Mobile, athletic and commanding, he is not a player any team lightly lets go, and some alleged Uruguay themselves had him banned, since Chile were opposed to . . . Uruguay. He was born on 25 October 1946, and his first World Cup was the 1966 series, in England. At one time the Brazilians were talking of naturalizing him, so well was he playing in their Championship, so badly did they need a centre-half, till the emergence of Pereira (q.v.), one of the few stoppers to match Figueroa in the 1974 competition. Now back in Chile.

Tom Finney (England). 'The Preston Plumber', so nicknamed for his second occupation, was unquestionably among the greatest English wingers there has been; it will always be a bone of contention as to whether he was superior to Stanley Matthews. Unquestionable it is that when Matthews played on the right wing, Finney on the left, England had some of their most stupendous games: a 10–0 victory over Portugal in Lisbon in May 1947, a 4–0 win against Italy in Turin a year later when Finney, cutting in from the wing, scored the last two goals. He was, indeed, a goal scorer, which Matthews never really was, a natural left-footed player who joined Preston from school as an inside-left, was converted to the right wing, and made his right foot as good as his left; he was adept at dancing outside the back and getting to the goal line. Already, in 1941, he was a young star, impressing everybody with his form in the League War Cup finals against Arsenal, but soon he was packed off in the Army to the Middle East, where he greatly impressed no less a right winger of the past than Alec Jackson (q.v.). The war years did nothing to blunt Finney's shining talent. He went straight into the England team, to the exclusion of Matthews, in 1946, and virtually stayed there, now on one wing, now the other, for a dozen years, winning seventy-six caps, scoring thirty goals, playing for Preston from 1940 to 1960. His balance was impeccable, his strategy subtle. At the end of his career he became a deep-lying centre-forward with

Preston, a role which he interpreted superbly, using his footwork to beat opponents, his two-footed shooting to score goals, his delicate distribution to make them. He was awarded the OBE and subsequently added journalism to his activities in the plumbing trade.

Brian Flynn (Wales). On one of their successful European Nations Cup away trips, in the 1974–6 tournament, Wales procured a high chair in their hotel and Terry Yorath, the captain, set Brian Flynn in it. He is a tiny fellow, but immensely courageous and exceptionally gifted, combative and quick, intelligent and ubiquitous, with great stamina. The more difficult the day, the better he is likely to be, as he showed especially in Zagreb when Wales lost to Yugoslavia in the Nations Cup quarter-final first leg in April 1976. Flynn, an ideal inside-forward, came to Burnley as a schoolboy from his native Port Talbot, made a couple of First Division appearances in season 1973–4 and twenty-three the season after. On 20 November 1974, he came on at Swansea against Luxemburg as substitute for John Mahoney; the following April, he appeared as a first choice in the Welsh side that beat Hungary in Budapest, and there he stayed. To stand 5 feet 2 inches and weigh $8\frac{1}{2}$ stone is not the ideal situation for a midfield player, but Flynn is good enough and brave enough to flourish just the same.

Just Fontaine (France). Fontaine arrived at the 1958 World Cup in Sweden expecting to be a reserve. He left an international star, scorer of thirteen goals, which is still a record, having figured in a tremendously fruitful partnership with Raymond Kopa (q.v.). Kopa, as deep-lying centre-forward, made the bullets, Fontaine fired them. Four of his goals came in the Third Place match at Gothenburg against the demoralized West Germans; his understanding with Kopa had the quality of radar. Kopa made the through pass, and there was the dark, stocky Fontaine haring after it, ahead of a defence which could never catch him, banging the ball finally past the goalkeeper with either, powerful foot. Born in 1933 in Morocco, he was brought into French football by Nice. He played centre-forward for France against Hungary in Budapest in October 1957, but then lost his place till the following March, when he again led the attack, against Spain in Paris, scoring a goal. He stayed in the team against Switzerland, but there was still no reason to expect what happened when France opened their World Cup programme against Paraguay in Norkopping on 8 June 1958; a 7–3 victory in which Kopa scored three goals; the first two in reply to that with which Paraguay took the lead. His career lasted until 1960 and brought him twenty caps, while in 1959 he moved to Reims, playing against Kopa when Real beat them in the 1959 European Cup Final in Stuttgart, resuming their partnership when Kopa came back to Reims. A leg twice broken ended his career, but he went on to become President of the French Footballers' Union, briefly manager of France, then manager of Paris Saint Germain.

Trevor Ford (Wales). A large, strong, dashing, highly physical but skilled centre-forward, originally a full-back, Ford was born in Swansea, played as a guest during the war for London's Clapton Orient at inside-right, joined Aston Villa in 1947, had three successful years there, then went to Sunderland at a record fee in 1950, where his partnership, if that is the word, with Len Shackleton (q.v.) was a somewhat eventful one. In 1953–4 he returned to Wales; to Cardiff City. Won the first of his thirty-seven Welsh caps in the 1945–6 Victory international against Ireland, his last in 1956–7. His last two clubs were PSV Eindhoven in Holland and Newport County. His total of Football League goals was 177.

Neil Franklin (England). On the eve of the 1950 World Cup in Brazil, Neil Franklin, twenty-seven, England's elegant and irreplaceable centre-half for the past five years, decamped to Bogota to play for the Santa Fe club. Colombia were then not members of FIFA, and there was nothing to be done. Franklin had previously withdrawn from the England team on the grounds that his wife was having a baby. He went to earn more money – English professionals then were wretchedly paid – but it proved a disastrous move. He stayed only a few months with his Stoke City friend and colleague, George Mountford, before cutting his losses and returning home. Stoke wanted no more of him and, after a suspension, he was transferred to Second Division Hull City. England, for whom he had first played in 1945 when serving in the Royal Air Force, and for whom he had won twenty-five full caps as well as four wartime and six Victory honours, never chose him again. He had turned professional with Stoke City in April 1949, having been born in Stoke itself. He was a very proper successor in the England team to Stanley Cullis (q.v.) being, like Cullis, essentially a gifted footballer first, a stopper second. Later he played for Crewe Alexandra, then became a coach and manager, in places as far apart as Cyprus and Colchester; but the flight to Bogota was the watershed of what till then had been such a distinguished career.

Robert Gadocha (Poland). An outside-left, bald, strongly built, very fast, a strong left-footed shot, a dangerous header of the ball, who was one of the best forwards of the 1974 World Cup. The following season, having been refused permission by the Polish FA to go to Bayern Munich, he was eventually allowed to leave his club, Legia Warsaw, and join Nantes in the French League. Gadocha was born in Cracow on 10 January 1946. He helped Poland to win the Olympic Football Tournament in Munich in 1972, then to win their World Cup qualifying group at the expense of England, but it was not until Lato (q.v.) gained a place in the team during that tournament that we saw Gadocha at his dangerous best. Surprisingly, he himself did not score in the World Cup Finals, but he was at the back of several of the seven goals that made Lato the leading scorer, with his rapid bursts, switching of wings, clever crosses and insidious corners. Off the field, Gadocha is a modest and amenable man. On it, he is not a player to be crossed with impunity. Wales found that out somewhat painfully in the World Cup qualifying competition in Katowice. Joined the Besiktas (Turkey) in 1977.

Hughie Gallacher (Scotland). It must ultimately be a matter of personal choice, but there are those who think little Hughie Gallacher was the best centre-forward of all time. A stormy petrel, forever in and out of difficulties, easily and often provoked on the field, dying a grim death when he killed himself on a railway line, he was yet the most artistic of leaders. He was immensely elusive, very fast, a splendid shot. He scored 365 goals in first class football, among them five for Scotland against Ireland in Belfast in 1929, five for the Scottish League against the Irish League, also in Belfast, in season 1924–5, when he also netted thirty-two for Airdrieonians. Born, like Alex James (q.v.), in Bellshill, he played splendidly for Newcastle United between December 1925 and May 1930, when Chelsea paid £10,000, a huge fee then, to bring him to London. Newcastle themselves had paid only half that sum, and Gallacher had scored 160 League goals for them, beginning with a double. In April 1929, he led the brilliant Wembley Wizards attack which scored five goals against England. He went on from Stamford Bridge to play for Derby County, Notts County, Grimsby Town and Gateshead. He was capped twenty times for Scotland.

Garrincha (Brazil). Real name: Manoel Francisco dos

Santos. 'Garrincha' is the name of a small bird. With his left leg distorted from an operation he had soon after birth, there could scarcely have been a less likely soccer hero than Garrincha. But the 5 foot 8 inches right winger made his apparent defect work for him, perfecting an insidious swerve round the outside of the full-back which was the equal of anything deployed by Stanley Matthews and adding to it a pantherine burst of speed. It was these attributes which allowed him twice to ridicule the left flank of the Swedish defence in the World Cup Final of 1958 in Stockholm, laying on two goals for Vavà (q.v.) which turned the game. He had been almost reluctantly brought into the Brazilian team for the third match, in Gothenburg against Russia, at the behest of his fellow players. Garrincha tore the Russian defenders to pieces, Brazil won 2–0, and he stayed in the team. In 1962, in Chile, he had added to these gifts a thundering left-footed shot and an astonishing ability in the air, outjumping the towering Maurice Norman, England's centre-half, to head a goal from a corner in the quarter-final in Viña del Mar. He got another with a glorious, deceptive, swerving shot from long range, and paved the way for Vavà to score when his free kick rebounded from Ron Springett, the England goalkeeper's, chest. Against Spain, in a decisive eliminating match on the same ground, he had been Brazil's saviour, when they seemed likely to lose the game. Against Chile, in the semi-final in Santiago, he was again wonderfully effective, scoring with a twenty-yard left-footer after nine minutes, heading in a corner for the second. Alas, he ended the game by being sent off for a retaliatory foul and had his head cut open by a bottle as he went. He was allowed by the disciplinary committee to play in the Final in which, by contrast with the previous games and with the 1958 match, he was oddly subdued. Father of seven daughters, he now left his wife and went off with a well-known Brazilian singer. A knee badly hurt in a motor accident still could not finish his career, and he actually played two games for Brazil's 1966 World Cup team in England, scoring a marvellous, characteristic goal from a free kick against Bulgaria. But by now the matchless acceleration, the famous elasticity, had inevitably gone. By then he had left Botafogo of Rio, whom he had joined in 1953, for the Corinthians of Sao Paolo. Born at Pau Grande in the State of Rio on 28 October 1933, he first played for the local club, and won over seventy caps.

Francisco Gento (Spain). 'Paco' Gento, as he was known, was one of the fastest and most dangerous left wingers of his period. He was an essential link in the splendid Real Madrid team which won the first five European Cups, combining beautifully with Di Stefano (q.v.) and was still in the team in 1966 when it beat Partizan in the Final in Brussels to win the sixth European title. Short, dark, well built, a champion sprinter in boyhood, Gento was born in 1933 at Guarnizo, Cantabrique, played for the local side Nueva Montana and went from there to Real after spells with Astillero and Santander. It was in 1953 that he arrived in Madrid, and his first season was a poor one. 1955, however, saw him win his first cap, against England in Madrid, and play ebulliently in the Latin Cup Final against Belenenses of Lisbon; it was in those days still an important competition. Gento was launched; he would win more than forty caps, play all three games for Spain in the Chilean World Cup of 1962, and two out of three, at the age of thirty-three, in the English version, in 1966. He scored for Real against Fiorentina in the European Cup Final of 1957, got the winner after 107 minutes against Milan in the 1958 Final. Renowned for his acceleration, his pastimes were hunting and fishing.

De Figureido Germano (Portugal). 'He *bounces* with energy,' said Walter Winterbottom, then the England team manager, of this marvellously resourceful and spectacular centre-half, tall and dark and bald with swashbuckling moustaches. Germano, however, was a curiously late developer, and injuries saw to it that he did not stay very long at the top, where he so palpably belonged. Born in Lisbon, he joined Benfica in 1960 for a mere £2,000 from the Atletico club, then in the Second Division. He was Benfica's centre-half when they won the European Cup Finals of 1961, against Barcelona, and 1962, against Real Madrid, but was then put out of the game for a year with a cartilage operation. On his return he helped Benfica to their fourth Final – having missed that of 1963 – but had to go in goal in Milan against Inter when Costa Pereira (q.v.) was hurt. He did not let through a goal, despite appalling, wet conditions. Germano was strong, fast, calm, athletic and extremely mobile. He won over twenty Portuguese caps, but alas his international career had ended by the time they reached the 1966 World Cup Finals. As well, perhaps, for England, who beat Portugal by only 2–1 in the semi-finals.

Gerson (Brazil). Short, stocky, very powerful in the thighs, puffing away at forty cigarettes a day, Gerson was Brazil's consummate midfield general in the World Cup of 1970, his immaculate left foot winging the ball vast distances with total accuracy. It was a consolation indeed for the poor World Cup he had had in England in 1966, when he played but a single game, against Hungary, and for the 1974 tournament, in which he couldn't play at all, a bad injury in a trivial indoor match having put him out of action. Born at Niteroi on 11 January 1941, he made his name in Rio with the Flamengo club, moving from there to Botafogo, and then to Sao Paolo, of that city, early in 1970. As a nineteen-year-old, he took prominent part in the Olympic Games tournament in Rome in 1960, but it is for 1970 he will be remembered; not least for the wonderful left-footed goal out of the blue, and from outside the box, with which he restored the

Brazilian lead, early in the second half of the World Cup Final. For all the power of Jairzinho, the mastery of Pelé, it was Gerson and his studied passing which bound that fine team together. Like so many Brazilians, he was a formidable taker of free kicks, imparting both power and swerve.

Alcide Ghiggia (Uruguay and Italy). The decisive forward of the 1950 World Cup decider against Brazil, it was little, hunched Chico Ghiggia who got away twice on the right wing with tremendous speed, once to make the equalizing goal for Schiaffino, then to score, with a tremendous right-foot shot, the winner. Brazil, before 200,000 astonished fans, were beaten. In May 1953, he left Montevideo and his club, Penarol, for Roma, making his debut for them in a friendly against Charlton Athletic. He was never quite the same player in Italy, but he played, on the usual dubious grounds of descent, five games for the Italian national team, the first against Portugal in Lisbon in May 1957, the last against Spain as late as 28 February 1959. A frail-looking little fellow, he lasted, in the bruising Italian Championship, a great deal longer than might have been expected; his pace, close control and powerful right-footed shot made him always capable of scoring a decisive goal; though none so decisive as that in Rio in 1950. He was born in Montevideo on 22 December 1926.

Johnny Giles (Republic of Ireland). In 1976, Johnny Giles, in his first season as player–manager of West Bromwich Albion, brought them back to the First Division. As player–manager of Eire, he had long coaxed the team to give far more than the sum of its component parts. A Dubliner, small, stocky, an admirable user of the flighted free kick, the floated long pass, and forever turning up in space to help colleagues under pressure, his partnership in midfield with Bremner (q.v.) was the motivation of Leeds United's success.

Giles played for them when they won the League, FA Cup, Fairs Cup, and appeared for them too in the Cupwinners' Cup (1973) and European Cup (1975) Finals, when only bizarre refereeing prevented them from winning. Born in Dublin, he came to Manchester United as a boy, developed into both a very good outside-right and a shrewd inside-forward, but left the club when things seemed to turn sour after United had been knocked out of the 1964 FA Cup semi-finals against West Ham. Leeds nipped in to sign him for £30,000, kept him out on the right wing at first, then put him where they had always intended; as successor in midfield to another mighty little man, Bobby Collins. Tough, resourceful, unspectacular but always influential, Giles was greatly missed when he left Leeds in 1975, after over a decade of diligent service. Became Shamrock Rovers manager in 1977.

Gilmar (Brazil). A calm and elegant goalkeeper who materially helped Brazil to win the World Cups of 1958 and 1962, and stayed on, a veteran, to play a couple of games in England in the less successful World Cup of 1966. Dos Santos Neves, to give him his correct name, was born in Santos, on 22 August 1930, but it was the Corinthians of Sao Paolo whom he initially joined in 1951, and not till ten years later did Santos sign him; for a ludicrous £1,000. In 1953 he succeeded the black Barbosa as Brazil's keeper in the South American Championships, but he didn't play in the World Cup, and it was only on the 1956 tour of Europe, when he saved penalties against England and Portugal, that he made sure of his place. Thereafter, handsome, grey-jerseyed and serene, he had a run of almost a decade, gymnastic when he had to be, but by and large so well positioned that heroics were unnecessary; precisely the player to give serenity to his defence. With Santos, he took part in the South American and Intercontinental Cup triumphs of the early 1960s.

Roy Goodall (England). A fine England captain, never better than when he rallied his defence in Rome in 1933, blood running from a cut above his eye, Goodall was one of the best of Huddersfield's traditionally fine full-backs. He played on the right, a hard tackler, always quick to the man and the ball, mobile and commanding. Born at Dronfield Woodhouse, near Sheffield, he joined Huddersfield in 1922 and played over 400 games for them in thirteen seasons, while winning twenty-five caps for England. Later he became Town's trainer.

Jimmy Greaves (England). Though he did not show at his best in a World Cup, and was bitterly distressed at being left out of the 1966 World Cup Final, Greaves was one of the most extraordinary British goal-scoring forwards of the postwar years. Small but sturdily built, his initiative, his terrific pace, his left-footed shot, his control, above all, perhaps, his almost telepathic flair for knowing where to be in and around the goalmouth, brought him 357 League goals. He was leading First Division scorer for Tottenham in season 1962–3 with thirty-seven goals, and again in 1968–9 with twenty-seven – an indication of how much defences had tightened, how hard it now was to get the half-the-length-of-the-field solo goals he once had scored; though the Total Football of the latter 1970s brought such goals back again. Greaves was born on 20 February 1940, in Poplar, East London, joined Chelsea from school, became a youth international, made an exciting debut against Spurs at White Hart Lane in August 1957, when he was seventeen, finished the season as Chelsea's leading scorer with twenty-two goals. He won the first of his fifty-eight England caps in an inauspicious game against Peru in Lima in 1959, when England lost, 4–1; in those games he scored no fewer than forty-four goals, and though Bobby Charlton eventually overtook him with forty-nine, it required nearly twice as many matches to do so. In May 1961, Greaves was transferred to Milan; most reluctantly, for he had second thoughts almost as soon as he had signed the contract. Though he continued to score goals – nine in ten games – even in the highly defensive Italian Championship, he was thoroughly unsettled there, perpetually in discord with the club and its unfamiliar disciplinary demands. At the end of the year he came back to London, and Tottenham Hotspur. Milan, who had paid only £80,000 for him, received just under £100,000. Greaves quickly helped Tottenham to retain the FA Cup, but in Chile the following summer he had a thoroughly disappointing World Cup. It looked as if he might do better in 1966 after he had thrown off a debilitating attack of jaundice. He scored four goals against Norway in Oslo on the run in to the World Cup, but was injured in the third match against France, and thereafter could not recapture his place from Geoff Hurst (q.v.). He concluded his First Division career with West Ham United, whom he joined in March 1970 in a deal involving Martin Peters (q.v.), though he emerged to play a handful of non-League games in 1976.

Gunnar Gren (Sweden). Nicknamed 'The Professor' in Italy, Gren was a lean, studious-looking inside-right who played a great part in Sweden's Olympic football success of 1948, and in 1958 was still good enough to be a star of the side which reached the Final of the World Cup in Stockholm. In the intervening years, the fact that he had turned full professional in Italy, a brilliant member of the all-Swedish Gre-no-li (Gren-Nordahl-Liedholm) trio for Milan, prevented his representing Sweden. He had a marvellous eye for the telling pass, excellent technique, and a very good right-footed shot; as he showed when he banged in a splendid goal against West Germany in his native Gothenburg, in the semi-final of the 1958 World Cup. Born there on 31 October 1920, he played for the IFK club, was transferred to Milan in 1949, helped them to win the Championship in 1951, joined Fiorentina of Florence in 1953, and was a key figure in their strong bid for the Championship that season. In 1955 he moved again to Genoa, in 1957 returned to Gothenburg, still a notably effective player, even in his late thirties, a testimony both to his virtuosity and his fitness. Later, he managed Juventus, of Turin.

Arthur Grimsdell (England). Reckoned one of the best English wing-halves of all time, Grimsdell was a very powerful man, one of whose specialities was to leap in the air, on a winter's afternoon, and bring the heavy, muddy ball of those times down with his broad chest. Charlie Buchan (q.v.) considered him the best footballer ever to play for England. A strong, clean tackler, very quick over short distances, he joined Tottenham Hotspur from his local team, Watford, in 1912, made over 300 appearances for them in first class football, captained the side which won promotion in 1920 and the Cup in 1921, played eight times only for England, including two Victory internationals in 1919. A captain who believed in exhortation, he had seventeen years with Spurs before he moved to Clapton Orient in 1929. Later he became a director of Watford, while his very large son played . . . rugby for the Harlequins!

Gyula Grosics (Hungary). The admirable and adventurous goalkeeper of Hungary's great team of the 1950s, winners of the 1952 Olympic tournament, 6–3 conquerors of England at Wembley in 1953, unluckily beaten in the World Cup Final of 1954. He was there again in Sweden's World Cup in 1958, having survived a period of 'disgrace' when caught smuggling contraband; a long suspension and 'banishment' from the Honved to the Tatabanya mining club were his punishment. Strong and flexible, Grosics was known above all for his dashing forays beyond the penalty area to kick clear, thus becoming at times almost a sweeper-cum-goalkeeper. He began with the Dorog club, but was one of many star footballers transferred by command to the Honved, Army team. Altogether he won eighty-nine caps, he still looked an excellent goalkeeper at thirty-seven in Chile in the 1962 World Cup, and there is good reason to say that never since have the Hungarians adequately replaced him.

Aarie Haan (Holland). For reasons best known to themselves the Dutch ignored Aarie Haan after the 1974 World Cup, in which he did so well for them in the unaccustomed position of stopper-sweeper. They could certainly have used him to advantage in the 1976 Nations Cup Final in Yugoslavia, when his great brio, his zestful versatility, his eager attacking from midfield, might have made such a great difference. The previous month, May, he had had a fine second half for Anderlecht, his Belgian club, when they beat West Ham United in Brussels in the Final of the European Cup-winners' Cup. The fair-haired Haan was born on 16 November 1948, joined Ajax of Amsterdam as a schoolboy, a right-sided midfield player who came on for them as substitute in the 1971 European Cup Final against Panathinaikos at Wembley in the second half, and scored. By 1972 he was no mere substitute but a driving force in the team, winning another European Cup medal against Inter in Rotterdam, following this with a third in Belgrade in 1973, against Juventus. Perhaps Holland would have won the 1974 World Cup had Haan been free to play in midfield, but an injury to his Ajax colleague, the stopper Hulshoff, forced him to drop back. Alas, it was Haan whom Bonhof (q.v.) rounded to set up the winning goal in the World Cup Final, but he did little else wrong in the tournament. He then left Ajax, which was shedding stars at the time like so many autumnal leaves, and joined Anderlecht of Brussels. Haan has a teacher's diploma and speaks both French and English.

Kurt Hamrin (Sweden). A little outside-right with exceptional pace and ball control, Hamrin scored one of the most spectacular goals of the 1958 World Cup in Gothenburg, in the semi-final against West Germany, picking the ball up on the right touchline, feigning somnolence, then springing to life to dribble past man after man at speed before beating the goalkeeper. In the Final, alas, he was overplayed by Nilton Santos (q.v.), but till then his opportunism, his brave forays on goal, had been among the features of the tournament; he had scored both Sweden's goals against Hungary, and another in the quarter-final against Russia. Hamrin, a withdrawn figure, who had little to say off the field, was an exuberant forward on it. He played with his stockings rolled down, scorning kicks, and was surprisingly good in the air for one so small. He was born in Stockholm on 19 November 1934 and played originally for the AIK club, who sold him to Juventus of Turin in 1956. He was slow to settled down and when John Charles and Sivori (q.v.) arrived in 1957, Juventus lent him to Padova. Following his admirable World Cup, he joined Fiorentina of Florence where he played for nine years with immense success, scoring twenty-six goals in each of his first two seasons, and bringing his total of League goals for them ultimately to 150; not to mention eight for Juventus and twenty in one season for Padova. In 1967 he began anew with Milan and won further honours. He scored both goals for them in Rotterdam in May 1968, when they beat Hamburg in the Final of the Cupwinners' Cup, and was on the right wing again the following year when Ajax were beaten 4–1 in the European Cup Final.

Gerhard Hanappi (Austria). 'Engineer Hanappi', as he was known in Vienna, was a blond, sturdily built footballer of great versatility and gifts, certainly one of the finest Austrian internationals since the war. Born in Vienna in 1929, he made his name with the Wacker club of Vienna, and to acquire him, in 1950, Rapid Vienna not only had to pay a large sum but had to sacrifice to Wacker a foreign tour. He was certainly worth all that, an immaculate stylist whether as an old school attacking centre-half, a right-back keen to overlap, or a right-half. He even did well for club and country at centre-forward, winning ninety-six caps which would surely have been over 100 had he not fallen out with Karl Decker, then the team manager. Eight times Austrian Footballer of the Year, of which seven such honours were consecutively gained, Hanappi played for FIFA against England at Wembley in 1953, and was in Austria's 1954 World Cup team, placed third in Switzerland, as right-back. No matter where you played him, his technique, judiciously applied strength and strong right foot made him outstanding.

John Hansen (Denmark). Standing well over 6 feet, a tall, strong, lean inside-left, particularly brave and effective in the air, but a highly skilled performer on the ground, John Hansen was a member of the Danish team which took third place in the 1948 Olympic Games at Wembley. Born in Copenhagen on 24 July 1924, he left his original club, Frem, to turn professional with Juventus of Turin in 1948, after the Games, stayed there till 1954, then had an embattled but admirable season in Rome with Lazio, whom his goals did much to save from relegation. He also showed great loyalty to the still more embattled English manager, George Raynor. When he returned to Copenhagen it was to play again for Frem, and ultimately to become the successful local representative of Coca Cola whose business, he said, 'I run like a football team.'

Eddie Hapgood (England). Perhaps the finest left-back of the inter-war years, a player of immaculate technique and timing, a fine captain, an admirable positional player, the loyalist of club men, Hapgood was born in Bristol in 1909.

Bristol Rovers gave him a trial when he was eighteen – how superbly slow clubs were to pick up talent in those days! – and offered him terms which Hapgood refused. They wanted him to drive a coal cart in the summer; and Hapgood was driving a milk float. So it was that a month later, another surprise, it was non-League Kettering Town who signed him, taking him to the Midlands. There Arsenal spotted him, after only a dozen games, and took him to Highbury, where he stayed for the rest of a career which ended only in 1945. He worshipped the Arsenal manager, Herbert Chapman, had a very close, but ultimately convoluted, relationship with the trainer (later manager) Tom Whittaker, won five Championship and two Cup medals with Arsenal, besides playing on the losing side in the 1932 Final. For England he made his debut in Rome against Italy in May 1933, and with a brief parenthesis in season 1936–7, retained his place up to October 1943. All told, he gained forty-three caps, including the 'unofficial' war years, and captained his country thirty-four times. He was an impeccable sportsman, and had an almost boyish loyalty to his club which, alas, was not as fully reciprocated as it might have been. In 1946 he became manager of Blackburn Rovers, subsequently managed Watford and Bath, but wound up his working life running a hostel for atomic energy authority apprentices in Weymouth. He died in retirement in Leamington.

Sam Hardy (England). Recognized as the finest English goalkeeper up to the Great War, Hardy played twenty-four times for England, including the post-war Victory internationals, gaining his first cap with Liverpool in 1906, his last with Aston Villa, in 1920. Like his famous successor, Hibbs (q.v.), Hardy was small for a goalkeeper, quite unspectacular, a magnificent positional player. Charlie Buchan (q.v.) called him, quite simply, the best he ever played against: 'I never saw him dive full length to make a save. He advanced a yard or two and so narrowed the shooting angle that forwards usually sent the ball straight at him.' Born in Chesterfield, where goalkeepers seem to grow like mushrooms, he made his name with Liverpool, was picked up surprisingly cheaply by Aston Villa in 1912, and stayed with them till 1921, helping them to win two Cup Finals. Later he played for Nottingham Forest and Hartlepools, bringing his League appearances to over 500.

Johnny Haynes (England). An exceptional passer of the ball, especially with cross-field or through passes, Johnny Haynes was born in Edmonton, North London, in 1934, but it was Fulham of South West London whom he joined when he left school. Already he was well known, having given a superb performance as a tiny inside-left for England against Scotland at Wembley in 1950, when still only fifteen years old. Later he would grow to 5 feet 10 inches and weigh over 11 stone: he was, indeed, a powerful player. In 1954-5 he got into the England Under-23 team with immediate success, and gained the first of his fifty-six international caps, against Northern Ireland. He played in two World Cups, 1958 in Sweden and 1962, as captain, in Chile, but it could not be said he was seen at his best in either of them. His international career ended in 1962 after a serious motor accident in Blackpool, but he recovered to play again for Fulham; his only Football League club, and one whom he served with great consistency. In 1961, when Milan coveted him, they made him Britain's first £100-a-week player.

Willie Henderson (Scotland). A tiny outside-right with a low centre of gravity, audacity, great speed and exquisite control, rounded off by a strong right-footed shot, Henderson was born at Baillieston and joined Rangers in 1959. In 1962 he was capped for Scotland, one of the youngest players to be honoured, and continued to play for them till 1969, winning over twenty caps. In 1972 Rangers transferred him to Sheffield Wednesday, and he played a couple of seasons of Second Division football at Hillsborough. It was an ironic coincidence that the other tiny, brilliant Glaswegian outside-right, Jimmy Johnstone (q.v.) of Celtic, should be also transferred to a Sheffield club, United, in 1975.

Harry Hibbs (England). If Hardy was the outstanding pre-war England goalkeeper, then Hibbs was quite the best between the wars. Standing only 5 feet 9 inches, his judgement of angles and agility made his lack of height irrelevant. He was born in the Midlands at Wilnecote, near Tamworth, played for Tamworth Castle and joined Birmingham, his only major club, in the summer of 1934. England capped him twenty-three times between 1929–30 and 1935–6. Later he became manager of Walsall where he had much to do with the development of a splendid protégé in Bert Williams, who went on to play for Wolves and England.

Nandor Hidegkuti (Hungary). Hero of Hungary's rout of England at Wembley in November 1953; the first home defeat for England by a foreign team. Hidegkuti scored three goals that day, the first a beauty in the second minute, when he made himself space to shoot through a gap with a delightful feint. He was the perfect 'deep-lying' centre-forward, in that he was just as capable of going forward to score as of coming back to link. He was a tireless, highly effective member, the following year, of the Hungarian team which thrashed England 7–1 in Budapest then lost by 3–2 to West Germany in a World Cup Final they morally deserved to win. Well built, well balanced and extremely versatile, Hidegkuti was born on 3 March 1922, in Obuda Ujlak, a working-class quarter of Budapest, and learned his football in the streets. He joined the famous, now defunct, MTK club, which was forced to change its name to Red Banner, then changed back again after the 1956 Revolution; which saw Hidegkuti, unlike Puskas, Kocsis and Czibor (q.v.), stay on in Hungary and play, much diminished, in the 1958 World Cup. Later managed his old club, Vasas Gyoer, Fiorentina and Hungary.

Rudi Hiden (Austria and France). Nicknamed 'The Flying Baker', Hiden was goalkeeper of the Austrian Wunderteam of the 1930s, playing a spectacular game against England at Chelsea in 1932. Herbert Chapman wanted to sign him for Arsenal, but the labour regulations frustrated him, after the transfer fee to Wiener AC had actually been deposited in a Viennese bank. So it was that Hiden went to France, played for the Racing Club de Paris, took French nationality and was capped by his new country. Afterwards he wandered the world, even playing for a time in Russia, later managing several clubs in Italy.

Uli Hoeness (West Germany). Hoeness was still technically an amateur right winger when he helped West Germany to win the European Nations Cup in Brussels in 1972. Four years later, every inch an expensive pro, said to earn a basic £60,000 a year, his all-purpose striking was a central feature of the Bayern Munich team which won the European Cup, in Glasgow, for the third successive year, and the West German team beaten only on penalties by Czechoslovakia for the Nations Cup in Belgrade. Hoeness it was, alas, who missed the decisive penalty, but his value to club and country has been immense, transcending even the fact that it was he who gave away the penalty in the first minute of the 1974 World Cup Final by tripping Cruyff (q.v.). Hoeness went on to play a large part in Germany's recovery with his marvellously sustained long runs, a compound of pace, stamina and admirable control. Blond and sturdily built, he was born on 5 January 1952, can play in midfield as well as up front, and had one of his finest games for Bayern in the replayed European Final of 1974 against Atletico Madrid in Brussels when he scored two exquisite goals.

René Houseman (Argentina). One of the revelations of the 1974 World Cup, a natural, ambidextrous winger of minuscule physique but immense pace, skill and courage. Houseman ran circles round the Italian defence in Stuttgart, much helped by the fact that the Italians, inconceivably, had decided he was a midfield man and 'marked' him for twenty minutes with Capello, an inside-forward! Houseman scored a fine goal that evening. Born on 19 July 1953, he played in the Huracan attack with other famous internationals in Babington (q.v.) and Brindisi.

Geoff Hurst (England). One of the heroes of England's triumph in the 1966 World Cup Final when he set a record by scoring three fine goals, one with each foot and one with his head. The second, and England's third, was the goal which went in off the West German crossbar and bounced just the right side of the line; according to the Russian linesman. Others dispute it to this day, but there is no dispute about the power of Hurst's right-footed shot, nor of the left-footer which brought a sensational fourth goal for England in the closing seconds of play. The son of an Oldham Athletic player, born in Ashton-Under-Lyne, Hurst joined West Ham from school, came up through their youth teams as a wing-half, and at one point was very nearly transferred, before he made with such huge success the transition to striker. His virtues were many; apart from that of finishing. His great power, his ability in the air, his unselfish running to make space for others, his near-post combinations with Martin Peters (q.v.) rendered him a vital member of the 1966 England team. His debut was made, oddly enough, against West Germany at Wembley, only in February of that year. Later he went on the pre-World Cup tour, played poorly in Copenhagen, lost his place in the team, and regained it only for the quarter-final, when he headed a magnificent winning goal against Argentina – from Peters's centre. A member of the West Ham teams which, also at Wembley, won the Cup in 1964, the Cupwinners' Cup in 1965, he concluded his career with Stoke and West Bromwich Albion, having played heroically well for England in the 1970 World Cup; above all against West Germany in the semi-final at Leon, Mexico. Altogether he won forty-two caps.

Rinus Israel (Holland). Had perhaps his finest game as the exceedingly mobile sweeper of the Feyenoord team which beat Celtic in Milan in the European Cup Final of 1970. Israel it was who went up to head the equalizing goal for Feyenoord, and thereafter to play a crucial part in his team's superiority. Born in Amsterdam on 19 March 1942, he worked as a pavement layer, becoming a part-time pro with the local DWS team at twenty, winning the first of over forty caps for Holland in September 1964 against Belgium. Two years later when Feyenoord bought him for some £30,000, he at last became a full-time pro, but also bought a cigar store in Rotterdam. Sweeper or stopper, excellent in the air, unfailingly calm, he was a fine captain of Feyenoord.

David Jack (England). An inside-right of abundant gifts, with a glorious swerve which once enabled him to leave five opponents floundering to score a goal for Arsenal, David Jack was the first £10,000 transfer when he joined them from Bolton Wanderers in 1929. In his eight years since joining the Lancashire club from Plymouth Argyle, where his father was the manager, Jack had become one of the leading forwards in the country, scoring the first Cup Final goal at Wembley in the initial Final there in 1923, and the winning goal for Bolton against Manchester City in the Final three years later. To this he added another medal when Arsenal beat Huddersfield Town in 1930, besides helping them to win the League Championship in 1921 and 1923. He was a tall, elegant figure, mysteriously capped only nine times for England, scorer of 143 League goals for Bolton, 112 for Arsenal. He later became manager of Southend United and Middlesbrough, dying in September 1958.

Alec Jackson (Scotland). The hero of the Wembley Wizards, Scotland's brilliant 1928 team which thrashed England 5–1 in April at Wembley, Jackson scored three of their goals, with typical opportunism. At 5 feet 7 inches, he was the tallest player in the little forward-line. Born in Renton, he began with Dumbarton, but in the early 1920s was tempted to the United States where with his brother Wattie he played with enjoyment for Bethlehem Steel. He returned to join Aberdeen, and in 1925 he went to Huddersfield Town for six distinguished seasons. A spell with Chelsea was less successful for he never settled down in London, and in due course he moved into non-League football. He specialized in converting centres from the left-wing. Alas, he died during the war in a car crash in the Middle East, while on Army service. He won seventeen caps for Scotland.

Jairzinho (Brazil). An outside-right in the proper succession of Julinho (q.v.) and Garrincha (q.v.), Jairzinho played three World Cups for Brazil, the second of them, in Mexico in 1970, when he won a medal, being much the most distinguished. In 1966 in England he was used out of position on the left wing. In 1974 he was still a menacing figure, but inadequately supported. In 1970 his enormous power, tremendous acceleration and pulverizing right-footed shot rendered him a perpetual menace. He scored two spectacular goals in the opening match against the Czechs in Guadalajara, leaving the defence gasping in the rear, the winner against England, another against Rumania, a quarter-final goal against Peru, a semi-final goal against Uruguay, a fulminating goal in the Final against Italy. Botafogo of Rio first used him as a centre-forward with Garrincha on the right wing. He marked his international debut against Portugal in 1964's so-called Little World Cup with a dramatic goal. Serious operations on his leg hindered him in 1967, but he shook these off to return in splendour to the game. A spell with Olympique Marseille after the 1974 World Cup was relatively unsuccessful, and he went back to play in Rio.

Alex James (Scotland). Probably the outstanding creative inside-forward of the inter-war years, certainly the indispensable general of the successful Arsenal team. An inside-left, small but solidly built, James was born in Bellshill, began his career in the famous Raith Rovers attack with Hughie Gallacher (q.v.), transferred in 1926 to Preston North End, was a member of the Wembley Wizards attack that scored five goals against England in 1928, and joined Arsenal the following year for £9,000. Somewhat against his will he was persuaded by their manager Herbert Chapman to become the deep-lying midfield pivot. His superb passing, either the through ball to a galloping centre-forward, the powerfully struck cross-field pass to the speeding Joe Hulme, or the pass inside the back to his left winger Cliff Bastin (q.v.), kept Arsenal's attack incisively on the move. He had exceptional ball control, fluttered his foot tantalizingly over the ball, deceived opponents with a subtle swerve. Only an occasional scorer, he did, however, get the first goal of the 1930 Cup Final for Arsenal after quickly taking a free kick, and a return from Bastin, but altogether scored for them only twenty-six in 231 League games. For Preston, by contrast, he got fifty-three in four seasons. Eight times capped for Scotland, captain of Arsenal for five years, he retired in 1953, died in June 1957.

Leighton James (Wales). Derby County paid Burnley, who had signed him from school, £300,000 for this red-headed winger in 1975. With his flowing run, his acceleration, his ability to beat opponents down the line on either flank, James had already established himself as one of the most dangerous attackers in Europe, playing a large part in Wales's qualification for the Nations Cup quarter-finals. Won his first cap in 1972, and has been a regular selection ever since.

Pat Jennings (Northern Ireland). Born in Newry, Jennings was a latecomer to professional football, working initially as a forester. He then joined Newry Town, played splendidly for Northern Ireland at Wembley in the 1963 European Youth Tournament, and was shrewdly acquired by Watford. Tottenham Hotspur signed him in 1964 after he had won his first cap, against Wales. In due course he replaced Bill Brown as their goalkeeper, while steadily remaining first choice for Northern Ireland, ultimately breaking Danny Blanchflower's record of appearances and, in 1976, passing Ted Ditchburn's appearance record for Spurs. A large, powerful man with huge hands, Jennings is at the same time tremendously agile, can hurl himself across goal to make saves which would incur the envy of any gymnast, or high diver. He is also adept at coming out to block with his legs, in what was initially the Continental way, and his right-footed goal kicks travel vast distances. In fact he once actually scored with a kick from hand against Manchester United at Old Trafford in the Charity Shield. He has won Cup Final and UEFA Cup medal with Spurs. Joined Arsenal in 1977.

Hans Jeppson (Sweden). Made his name in the opening match of the 1950 World Cup in Sao Paolo for Sweden against Italy when he turned the illustrious Carlo Parola, Italy's centre-half, inside out, scored twice, and enabled Sweden to qualify for the Final Pool. The following season he spent a few months in England studying office furniture design, played for Charlton Athletic as an amateur, and transformed their attack. He got a hat trick against Arsenal in February 1951 when Jack Kelsey made his unhappy debut in goal, and was presented with the ball by Arsenal. He then turned professional with Atalanta of Bergamo in the Italian League, and moved on the following season to Naples, where he stayed for many successful years, marrying the daughter of a rich local businessman. A tall, lean, strong centre-forward, effective rather than subtle, Jeppson was born on 10 May 1925, in Kungsbacka, played for the Djurgarden club, and was intensively coached by little George Raynor from Yorkshire when he was national coach in Sweden.

Bob John (Wales). One of the best and most versatile footballers to play for Wales and a crucial member of the Arsenal team which established ascendancy in the early 1930s, Bob John was best known as a left-half. Arsenal managed to outwit Cardiff City to sign him in 1922, after he had made a name outside the League with Barry Town and Caerphilly. His fifteen international caps spanned a fifteen-year period, he became a makeshift left winger to score Arsenal's goal in the 1932 Cup Final, he won a medal for them in the 1930 Final, and three Championship medals besides. A calm, resourceful, highly efficient player, excellent in his distribution.

Jimmy Johnstone (Scotland). Perhaps the most talented and certainly the most spectacular and controversial member of the fine Celtic team which dominated Scottish football for ten years in the 1960s and 1970s, reaching two European Cup Finals, winning one of them, little, red-haired Johnstone was an outside-right of extraordinary talent. With his low centre of gravity, his speed, his marvellous close control, his ability to go past the full-back either way, his courage in attempting it, he carried the banner for true wingers at a time when they were unfashionable. Often he was cruelly maltreated, not least by the thugs of Buenos Aires's Racing Club in the notorious world club championship series of 1967: in the Montevideo match he had to wash the spittle out of his hair at half-time. A law unto himself, Johnstone had many ups and downs both with Celtic and the Scotland team – on one occasion, at Largs, he drifted out to sea in a boat and had to be rescued. But there was never any doubt of his bravery and virtuosity. Of his many splendid appearances for Scotland, perhaps the finest was in 1966 at Hampden, when England's defence could do nothing with him as he beat them constantly down the line. In 1975 he joined Sheffield United on a free transfer, but this was the merest postscript to his fine career.

Julinho (Brazil). The best outside-right in the coruscating 1954 World Cup, scorer of what was perhaps the best goal with a colossal right-footed drive from outside the box against Hungary in Berne, Julinho later went from Portuguesa of Sao Paolo to Fiorentina, whom he materially helped to win the Italian Championship of 1955–6; their first. A somewhat brooding and bronze figure, he was a compound of remarkable close control, electric pace and great power. Christened Giulio Botelho, born in Sao Paolo on 5 August 1929, he returned to Brazil, and the national team, in the summer of 1959; and promptly demolished the England defence in Rio.

Josip Katalinski (Yugoslavia). A centre-half of the most modern variety, eager, sometimes to a fault, to go up to score goals as well as stop them, Katalinski was a major force in the 1974 World Cup, and in the Finals of the 1976 Nations Cup in his native Yugoslavia. There he scored a goal, almost had a couple more, kicked off the line, took infinite risks. Caution is anathema to this tall, strong player, excellent in the air with a thundering right-footed shot. Born in 1948, making his name and fame with his local club Zeljeznicar Sarajevo, playing basketball effectively besides football (he believes that footballers should practise other sports), he helped Zeljeznicar win the Yugoslav Championship in 1973, scored the play-off goal against Spain in Frankfurt which took Yugoslavia into the World Cup Finals of 1974, joined OGC Nice in the summer of 1975, took his total of caps to thirty-nine in the Nations Cup finals.

Kevin Keegan (England). 1976 saw him establish himself as one of the most dangerous and versatile strikers in the game, much coveted by Real Madrid, the outstanding member of a Liverpool team which won both the Championship and the UEFA Cup, an ebullient figure in the England attack. Born in Armthorpe, Yorkshire, he was turned down after a trial with Coventry City, and came home to find he could not even win a regular place in his works team. But Scunthorpe United offered him terms, he established himself there as an outside-right of promise, and Bill Shankly bought him for Liverpool from the Fourth Division club in 1971, after he had made forty-five appearances and scored nine goals for them the previous season. With Liverpool, Keegan matured into a player of exceptional versatility, small but muscular and very quick, increasingly intelligent, a brave darter into striking positions, unexpectedly good in the air, a strong right-footed shot, quick and neat in tight circumstances. His first appearances for England, in 1973, were unimpressive, but on the summer tour of 1974, despite a brutal beating up by airport police in Yugoslavia, he showed what he could do at this level. He kicks a dead ball with immense force, as he showed when scoring from a free kick against Bruges in the 1976 UEFA Final; his second successful one with Liverpool. In the 1977 European Cup Final in Rome, he excelled. Then he joined Hamburg.

Fred Keenor (Wales) Winning thirty-two international caps for Wales, Keenor was a splendid centre-half whose career spanned the Great War. Cardiff-born, he helped them win promotion to the First Division in 1921, and captained them when they beat Arsenal in the Cup Final of 1927. In 1931 he left Cardiff City for Crewe Alexandra, then moved into non-League football as player-manager of Tunbridge Wells Rangers in 1935–6; when his prestige was still great enough to have him included in a cigarette card series! Played more than 400 League games for Cardiff. Perhaps his finest match for Wales was at Ibrox against Scotland in 1930, when he inspired a team patched together at the last moment from obscure, even non-League, players to hold Scotland 1–1.

Bob Kelly (England). An outstanding inside-right of the 1920s, 'noted for his swerve and quick burst', wrote Charlie Buchan (q.v.), himself a great inside-right, who put Kelly in his ideal post-1925 team. Made his name in the famous Burnley team which won the Championship in 1920–21, setting up a long-standing record for an undefeated run. Won twelve caps with Burnley, two more with Huddersfield Town, for whom he formed a famous right wing with Alec Jackson (q.v.).

Jack Kelsey (Wales). Perhaps reached his peak as Wales's immaculate goalkeeper in the World Cup Finals of 1958 when they reached the quarter-finals, scaring Brazil, and he attributed his safe handling to . . . chewing-gum: 'Always put some on my hands. Rub it well in.' His hands were large, he had once been a blacksmith, brought up in the little village of Winch Wen. Arsenal summoned him to London, kept him waiting in their marble halls all day, but eventually signed him. He made his debut against Charlton Athletic at Highbury in February 1951, letting through five goals, but in due course established himself as a brave and agile goal-

An England team at the turn of the century, including (*ball between feet*) its amateur captain G. O. Smith (*Colorsport*)

Three great English forwards of the early 1930s: David Jack (*right*), Dixie Dean (*below right*) and Cliff Bastin (*below*) (*Colorsport*)

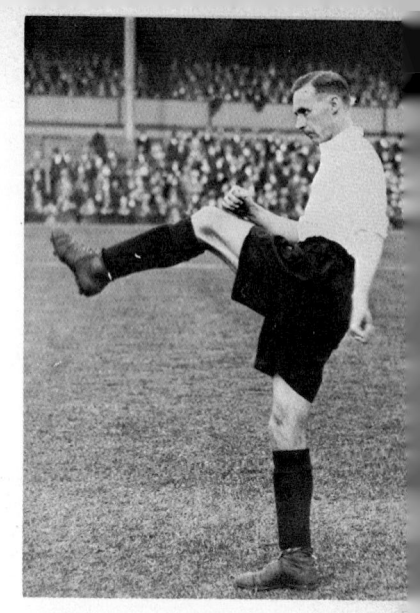

Two defenders from the Great War days: Bob Crompton (*left*), the best full-back of his time, and Charlie Buchan (*below*), an inside-forward who late in his career invented the Third Back game (*Colorsport*)

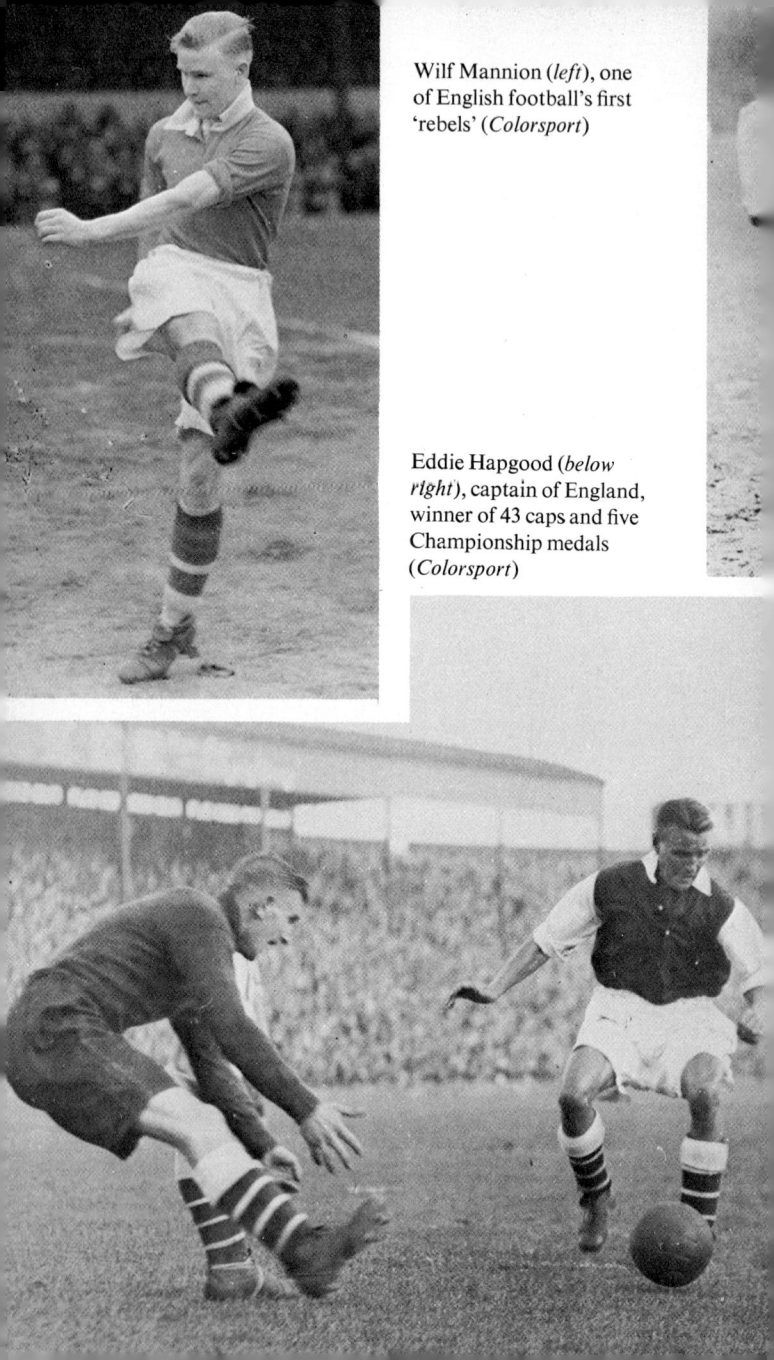

Wilf Mannion (*left*), one of English football's first 'rebels' (*Colorsport*)

Eddie Hapgood (*below right*), captain of England, winner of 43 caps and five Championship medals (*Colorsport*)

Tommy Lawton and John Charles (*inset*), prodigious goalscorers for a number of clubs (*Colorsport*)

Perhaps the two greatest English wingers of all time: Tom Finney (*below left*) and Stanley Matthews (*Colorsport*)

Danny Blanchflower (*top left*) in the shirt of Spurs whom he captained to the League and Cup double in 1961 (*Popperfoto*)

Bobby Moore and Bobby Charlton (*above*), between them holders of 214 English caps (*Colorsport*)

George Best (*left*): 'Technique, courage, pa< imagination... what fea he has performed!' (*Colorsport*)

Opposite: Team-mates i the Italian national side but Milanese club rivals Sandro Mazzola of Internazionale (*right*) an Gianni Rivera of A. C. Milan (*inset*) (*Colorsport*)

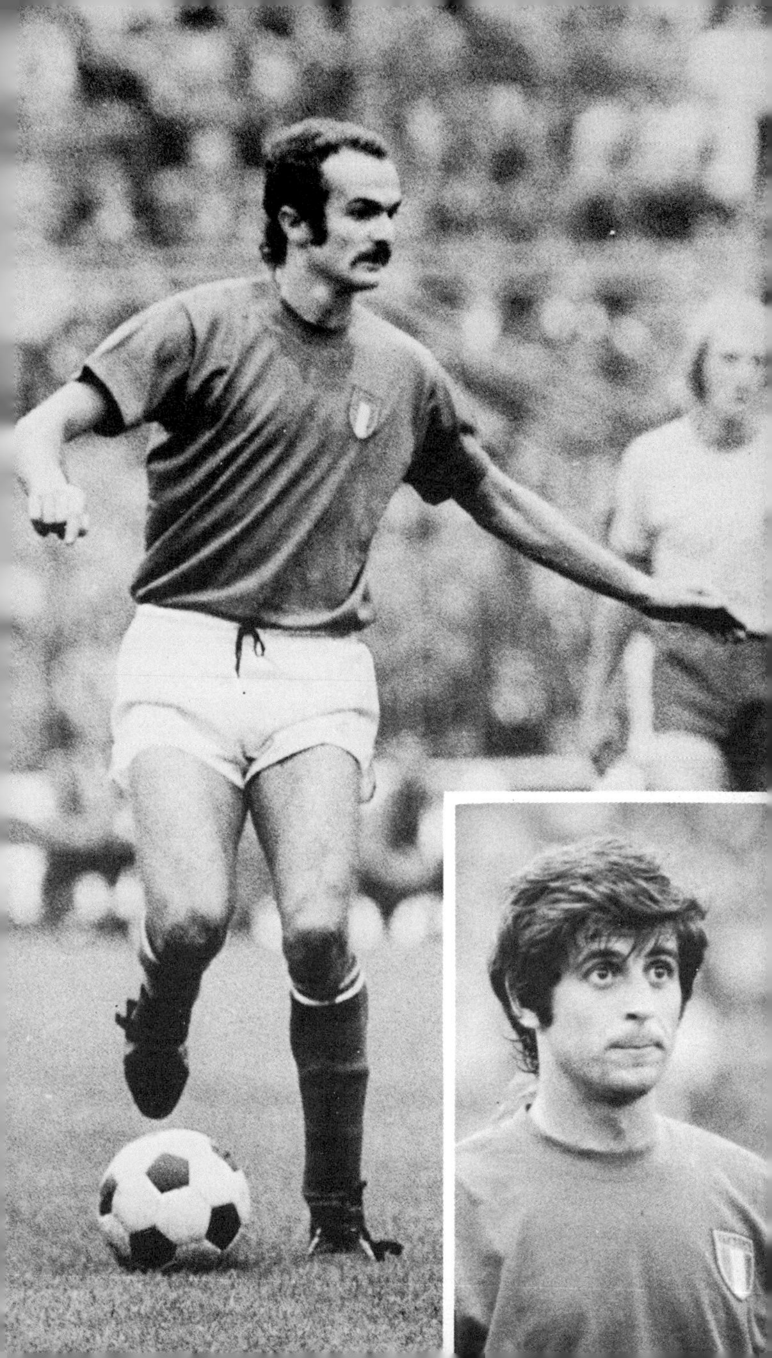

Lubanski and Gadocha lead Poland's celebrations after their victory in the 1972 Olympic Games final (*Colorsport*)

Oleg Blokhin, European Footballer of the Year in 1975 (*Colorsport*)

Meazza of Italy and Sarosi of Hungary (*top left*) before the 1938 World Cup Final (*Keystone Press*)

Raymond Kopa (*top right*), versatile French centre-forward (*Presse Sports*)

Didi (*above*), 'the peerless, creative inside-forward' from Brazil (*Presse Sports*)

Two centre-halves from the 1950s (*right*): Billy Wright of England and Ernst Ocwirk of Austria (*Popperfoto*)

Uruguay's Pedro Rocha (*centre*) in action against Mexico during the 1966 World Cup tournament (*Popperfoto*)

Alfredo Di Stefano (*left*), a superlative forward who could also defend (*Keystone Press*)

Luis Suarez (*right*), 'unquestionably among the best European inside-forwards of the 1960s' (*Popperfoto*)

Eusebio (*below*), the best Portuguese forward of all time (*Colorsport*)

Bulgarian forward Christo Bonev (*left*) (*Colorsport*)

Dino Zoff (*below*) kept the ball out of Italy's net for a record 1,143 minutes (*Colorsport*)

Josip Katalinski (*bottom left*), Yugoslav centre-half 'of the most modern variety' (*Colorsport*)

Three international stars:

Ralf Edstrom of Sweden (*left*), playing for PSV Eindhoven in the Dutch League (*Colorsport*)

Dragan Dzajic of Yugoslavia, then with the French club Bastia, and Scotsman Billy Bremner clash in the 1974 World Cup (*Colorsport*)

Brazilian centre-half Luis Pereira (*top left*) (*Colorspor*

Luigi Riva (*bottom left*): 'the most admired and incisive Italian forward since the war' (*Colorspor*

Pelé (*below*) in action during the 1970 World Cup Final against Italy: 'the finest player of his generation and perhaps the greatest of all time' (*Editôra Abril*)

Two outstanding footballers of the seventies: Johan Cruyff (*above*) of Holland and Franz Beckenbauer of West Germany (*Colorsport*)

keeper, acrobatic on the line, shrewd in his judgement, in season 1953–4. The first of his many Welsh caps came that season, and he played for Britain against Europe in Belfast in August 1955.

Alexei 'Tiger' Khomich (Russia). A spectacular goalkeeper who made a great impression on the famous Moscow Dynamo tour of Britain in 1945, Khomich was not very tall but he was strongly built and enormously acrobatic. He divided the goal into invisible zones, of which Spot 9, the top corners, were the most dangerous to him. On his retirement he became a Press photographer, who for the last twenty years or so has been found behind the goal rather than in it.

Ove Kindvall (Sweden). A star of the 1970 European Cup Final for Feyenoord of Rotterdam against Celtic in Milan, Kindvall had the previous year become only the second footballer ever to be voted Swedish Sportsman of the Year. First came to international prominence with two excellent goals scored for Sweden against Brazil in Gothenburg just before the 1966 World Cup when he was with his original club, Norkopping, famous for centre-forwards. The determined bursts were typical of his play. In 1969 two more goals scored against France qualified Sweden for the 1970 World Cup in Mexico, while he also played part of a game against Uruguay in the 1974 World Cup; by which time he had returned to Sweden. Not very large, but sturdily built, quick, brave, incisive, with a devastating change of pace, he was a prolific goal scorer with Feyenoord.

Lord Kinnaird (Scotland). As the Honourable A. F. Kinnaird, a formidable, red-bearded figure, he was one of the great pioneers of soccer, playing for Old Etonians, the Wanderers and, on the occasion of the first ever international match, for Scotland against England. Delighted in the practice of hacking. When his wife once expressed her fears to a friend that her husband might one day come home with a broken leg she was reassured, 'Don't worry, it won't be his own.' A hero of the early Cup Finals, he later became President of the Football Association.

Sandor Kocsis (Hungary). Nicknamed 'Golden Head' for his performance in the 1954 World Cup, when his remarkable jumping and astonishingly powerful heading brought spectacular goals. His total of eleven made him the tournament's leading scorer, though in the Final Hungary were so unexpectedly beaten by West Germany. Famous for his partnership as striking inside-forwards with Ferenc Puskas (q.v.) both for Honved and Hungary, Kocsis, like Puskas, stayed abroad after the Hungarian Revolution of 1956 and eventually joined Barcelona, with great success. Of no more than average height but with a thick, powerful neck, he was born in Budapest on 21 September 1929, and regularly wore out his shoes playing football in the streets. Not till he joined the junior team of the KTC club did he wear a real pair of football boots. From there he moved to his favourite team, Ferencvaros, which was subsequently, though temporarily, amalgamated with Honved. Played for Barcelona in the European Cup Final in 1961.

Ivan Kolev (Bulgaria). A small, dark forward who could play just as cleverly and efficiently at inside or outside-left. He began as the first, making a name for himself in the pre-Olympic tournament of 1956, but by the 1962 World Cup he was using his pace and skill as a left winger, partnered by his club colleague from the Army team of Sofia (CDNA then CSKA), Yakimov. Spanish clubs wanted him, but the Bulgarians would never let him go. Born in Sofia in the suburb of Ji Dimitri in 1931, the son of a chauffeur, his first club was Sportist, whence he moved first to VVC, the Air

Force side, then CDNA. He eventually became a major in the Army, specializing in physical education.

Raymond Kopa (France). One of the salient figures of the 1958 World Cup, in which his superlative play as a deep-lying centre-forward enabled France to take third place and Just Fontaine (q.v.) to establish a record by scoring thirteen goals. Born Raymond Kopaczewski at Noeux-les-Mines on 13 October 1931, the son of a Polish miner, Kopa was hurt in a mining accident, became a full-time pro, joined Angers, and from there went to his chief love, Reims. Initially an outside-right, he was capped by France there for the first time in 1952. Reims turned him into an all-purpose centre-forward; as such he inspired them to reach the first ever European Cup Final in 1956, playing so well against Real Madrid that they signed him. There the presence of Di Stefano (q.v.) forced him to play on the wing, where he won three consecutive European Cup Final medals, the third, ironically, against his old team Reims. But he was never happy playing second fiddle, his gifts of balance, vision, control and deadly passing fitting him ideally for the role he played in the 1958 World Cup. In 1959 he went back to finish his career with Reims. He won in all forty-five French caps, a small, neat, infinitely versatile figure.

Ruud Krol (Holland). One of the most gifted and omni-competent full-backs of his day, a left-back who forced Inter's goalkeeper to a spectacular save in the 1972 European Cup Final when overlapping on the *right*, Rudi Krol was born in Amsterdam on 23 March 1949, began his career with Rood Wit, and joined Ajax in 1967. A broken leg caused him to miss the European Cup Final of 1971, but he played in the next two, and had a fine World Cup in West Germany in 1974. Fast, strong and a player of exceptional pace and stamina, he is winger and full-back happily combined. Two more appearances in the Nations Cup Finals of 1976 in Yugoslavia brought his total of caps to forty-one.

Ladislao Kubala (Spain, Hungary, Czechoslovakia). That unique phenomenon, a *treble* international, a native Hungarian who also played for Czechoslovakia and, on escaping from behind the Iron Curtain and being naturalized, for Spain, whose national team manager he still was in 1976. He was actually born in Budapest on 10 June 1927, first played League football for Ferencvaros, was capped for Hungary, went to Bratislava for a spell and was capped by the Czechs, a centre or inside-forward of refined technique, enormously powerful thighs, a thumping right-footed shot. In 1950 he escaped from Hungary to Italy, where Pro Patria tried in vain to sign him. He toured South America with a team of other Iron Curtain countries' refugees, was banned by Hungary but signed in defiance of the ban by Barcelona, who were supported by the Spanish Federation. In due course he was naturalized, became a star of a multi-national Barcelona attack, playing in the 1961 European Cup Final in Berne against Benfica. In 1953 he played brilliantly for the Rest of the World against England at Wembley scoring two goals, one from the penalty spot. On retirement he became a coach with Barcelona, eventually managing their first team, but on dismissal went back to playing football for the other Barcelona side, Espanol, then, in the summer of 1967, for Toronto in the American USA League, before eventually taking over the Spanish national team. With Toronto, he played side by side with Branko, his son.

Angel Labruna (Argentina). A busy, gifted inside-left whose long career with River Plate of Buenos Aires featured a distinguished wing partnership with Loustau and brought him 457 goals in 1,150 matches, 293 of them in the League.

At his best he was a quick, penetrative player with excellent control; one remembers his fine run and cross from the left wing bringing Argentina's goal by Boyé when they first came to Wembley in May 1951. There can seldom have been a better club attack than that formed by Munoz, Morena, Pedernera, Labruna and Loustau which was known as 'The Machine', and was broken up only by the mass exodus of Argentinian players to Colombia in the late 1940s. Labruna didn't go. Born in 1917, he stayed on to make two signal returns to the national side; in 1955's South American Championships, and in the 1958 World Cup when, by now forty years old and nicknamed 'El Viejo' (the Old One), he still inspired them to beat Northern Ireland in Sweden.

Grzegorz Lato (Poland). One of the stars of the Polish team which took third place in the 1974 World Cup in Germany and leading scorer of the competition with seven goals (including that which beat Brazil in the third-place match), Lato was given his chance when the injured Lubanski (q.v.) dropped out of the team in 1973. A stockily built, very fast, mobile outside-right with great acceleration and a fine right-footed shot, he worked up a magnificent partnership with his fellow winger, Gadocha (q.v.). Born on 8 April 1950, he established himself with Stal Mielec, helping them to win the Championship of Poland in 1973 and again three years later.

Denis Law (Scotland). Born in Aberdeen in 1940, Denis Law at fifteen, when he joined Huddersfield Town, looked a blond, fragile schoolboy with glasses. There was little sign that he would develop into one of the most versatile and energetic inside-forwards of his day, a fine constructive player, a superb header of a ball, an acrobatic finisher. Manchester City paid £55,000 for his transfer in 1960, and sold him a year later to Torino for £100,000. He was greatly admired in Turin, where he played together with Joe Baker, from Hibernian, but he could not settle and, after a rather stormy season, came back to Manchester, United this time, in 1962, promptly helping them to win the FA Cup Final, giving a remarkable display. Later that year he had another dazzling game at Wembley, this time for the Rest of the World against England. An Indian Summer with Manchester City enabled him to bring his total of Scottish caps to a record fifty-four, and to play in the 1974 World Cup Finals against Zaire.

Tommy Lawton (England). Perhaps the most effective British centre-forward of his era, Lawton was leading the Burnley attack at sixteen, scored three against Spurs on his first appearance as a professional, was sold to Everton at seventeen for an unparalleled £6,500, as successor to Dixie Dean. Born in Bolton, like another fine centre-forward Nat Lofthouse, and once employed, like him, in Walker's Tanneries, he became England's centre-forward in 1938 at the age of nineteen, winning a Championship medal with Everton, and scored no fewer than thirty-five goals for them. Tall, a superb header of a ball who seemed to 'hang' in the air, a tremendous shot with either foot, a fine distributor, he headed the winning goal against Scotland at Hampden Park in April 1939, England's first victory there for twelve years. The war saw him playing for the Army, Aldershot, as a guest, and many times for England, for whom he scored four against Scotland at Maine Road in 1943, one goal being hooked over his head while he was sitting on the ground. In November 1945, Everton sold him to Chelsea, but in December 1947 he was on the move again; this time to Third Division Notts County, whom he would later manage, for a then record £20,000. In March 1952 he became player-manager of Brentford, in September 1953 he went briefly to Arsenal. He won twenty-three full England caps, scored 215 League goals.

Leonidas Da Silva (Brazil). Known always as 'Leonidas', a little black centre-forward who was one of the most spectacular players of the 1938 World Cup, famous for his bicycle kick, nicknamed 'The Black Diamond'. Began his career in Rio, left in 1933 to play in Montevideo for Penarol, returned in 1934 to win a Championship medal with Vasco da Gama of Rio, then after another year signed for Botafogo. Since that Rio club would seldom use a black player, he felt it to be a challenge. Initially an inside-right, he was foolishly rested from Brazil's team in the 1938 World Cup semi-final in Marseille, so confident were they that they would beat Italy. They didn't. In later years Leonidas became a radio reporter.

Nils Liedholm (Sweden). A member of the famous Grenoli trio of Swedish inside-forwards which played so well for Milan in the late 1940s, Liedholm, then an inside-left, dropped back to become a splendid right-half in the 1950s. Thoroughly versatile, good in the air as well as on the ground, a tall, strong, composed figure, he played outside-left in the Swedish team which won the 1948 Olympic title in London, inside-left in the team which played Brazil in Stockholm in the World Cup Final of 1958. Then, in the opening minutes, he picked his way elegantly through the Brazilian defence to score, but he was unable to add another gold medal to his Olympic one. It was, in fact, his second disappointment of the early summer, for he had been an outstanding member of the Milan team unluckily defeated after extra time by Real Madrid in the European Cup Final in Brussels. Born in Waldermarkvik on 8 October 1922, he predictably became a most successful manager in Italy, variously with Milan, Fiorentina and Roma.

Benito Lorenzi (Italy). Nicknamed 'Veleno' ('Poison'), and not without cause, Lorenzi was a centre or inside-forward of great gifts and all-round ability, a stupendous ball player with an excellent right-footed shot. A Tuscan born at Borgo Buggiano (Pistoia) on 20 December 1925, he joined Empoli in 1946, Internazionale of Milan in 1947, and there became a star. For Italy he played on fourteen occasions, the first being in Madrid in March 1949. Perhaps his finest game was against England in the Tottenham fogs of the following November, when he helped Italy gain an ascendancy they just couldn't translate into goals. He figured in the 1954 but not, most surprisingly, in the 1950 World Cup, an always explosive, often provocative but greatly gifted player.

Wlodek Lubanski (Poland). For all the fact he did not play in their famous World Cup team of 1974, Lubanski is still probably the best player Poland has ever produced; and they would not have got there without him. It was he who was the architect of Poland's World Cup victory over England in 1973, his last international game till 1976 and one in which he disastrously aggravated a knee injury. He provoked the controversial free kick from which the first Polish goal came, magisterially scored the second when robbing an over-confident Bobby Moore and running on alone to score. Well built, fair-haired, a beautiful mover and an elegant ball player, Lubanski had played twenty times for Poland before his twentieth birthday, and was the inspiration of the Gornik club. Then came the first setback in a curiously starcrossed career. He recklessly exceeded the prescribed dose of pills when recovering from an illness and was forced out of football for two years. His return was brief but brilliant. Born in 1947, he should still, by rights, be a leading international player; but he will be remembered. In 1975–6 he was sufficiently recovered to join the Lokeren club in the Belgian Championship, and his lively form enabled them to have an unexpectedly good season.

R. S. McColl (Scotland). One of the outstanding centre-forwards of pre-Great War days, McColl began with the famous Glaswegian amateurs Queens Park, was still with them when he knocked in three goals in twenty minutes against England at Celtic Park in 1900, and from there went on to Newcastle and Rangers. R. S. McColl is a name that stayed familiar in Glasgow long after his retirement, for he had a successful chain of tobacco stores. When Bob McColl turned up to join Queens Park at the age of eighteen, he was so small and slight that the doorman wouldn't believe he was a player, but his speed, swerve and tremendous shot in either foot made him exceptionally dangerous. Turning pro with Newcastle in 1901, he returned to Scotland to play for Rangers, and subsequently became one of only two players to be reinstated as an amateur with Queens Park. He was fourteen times capped for Scotland.

Bill McCracken (Ireland). The full-back who can be called responsible for the change in the offside law of 1925; his wily offside tactics made it inevitable that something be done, so shrewdly did he operate them with his partner, Hudspeth. Tremendously fast in both thought and movement, he joined Newcastle from Distillery in 1905 and stayed for eighteen years, winning twenty-three caps which would have been many more, had it not been for the Great War and a dispute he had with the Irish selectors. He became manager of Hull City and Aldershot, and was scouting still for Millwall until well into his nineties, a marvellous nonogenarian.

Danny McGrain (Scotland). A thoroughly modern full-back of great all-round ability, defensively sound, very fast, splendidly effective when he goes forward. He can play just as well on either flank, being at left-back in all three of Scotland's 1974 World Cup matches in West Germany, right-back when he had an outstanding British International tournament in 1976. After sporadic appearances in the previous two seasons, he won a regular place in the Celtic team in season 1972-3 and won his first three caps for Scotland in the British Championship in May 1973.

Jimmy McGrory (Scotland). Scorer of 550 goals in first class football, 410 of them in the Scottish League, seven times capped for Scotland, McGrory, though small, was the most prolific Scottish centre-forward between the wars. Strong and hard with a fine burst of speed and a great flair for taking chances, he was born in Glasgow and went to Celtic in 1922 from St Roch's, Clydebank. It was to Clydebank that he went on loan for a season in 1923-4, Clydebank whom he joined when he at last left Celtic in 1938, but he went back to Celtic in 1946 to spend nineteen years as their manager.

Jimmy McIlroy (Northern Ireland). An inside-right of great technical gifts and excellent distribution, McIlroy, with Danny Blanchflower (q.v.), made up the engine room of the fine Northern Ireland team which got to the quarter-finals of the 1958 World Cup in Sweden. Born in Largs, he established himself with Glentoran and joined Burnley for £7,000 at the age of nineteen. He was a great force in their League Championship season of 1959-60, linked admirably with his right-half, Jimmy Adamson, played in the Cup Final of 1962, was surprisingly sold to Stoke for £25,000 in 1963. Won fifty-three caps for Northern Ireland.

Jimmy McMullan (Scotland). A small but elegant left-half, famous for thirty and forty-yard passes, McMullan established himself with Partick Thistle, became an international in 1920, came south to Manchester City in 1926. In 1928 he was a splendid captain of the scintillating Wembley Wizards, completing a notable triangle with James and Morton (q.v.). Winner altogether of sixteen Scottish caps, he made the usual move in reverse when, in his last season, he moved up to inside-left for City and played there in the 1933 Cup Final.

Archie Macaulay (Scotland). Born in Falkirk, the red-haired Macaulay joined Glasgow Rangers from Camelon Juniors and was a Scottish Cup and League medal winner when he impressed London by playing well against Rangers, and joined West Ham for £6,000. How Rangers must subsequently have regretted it, just as West Ham must have regretted selling him to Brentford in 1946. During the war, on Army service, he played as a guest for Doncaster Rovers, dropped back from inside-left to right-half, allied a biting tackle to his creative skills, won a place in the Scotland team, and became an outstanding half-back. In May 1947 he played for Britain against the Rest of Europe at Hampden, soon afterwards being transferred to Arsenal, whom he promptly and materially helped to win the Championship in 1947–8. After 103 League games at Highbury he was sold to Fulham, later becoming manager of Guildford City, Norwich City and Brighton.

John Mahoney (Wales). A compactly built, curly-headed midfield player – an inside-right one would call him in traditional parlance – who had much to do with Wales's successful run in the 1976 European Nations Cup. His energy, bite, intelligence, control and nice distribution made him the first really authoritative Welsh creative player since Ivor Allchurch (q.v.). Cardiff-born but brought up in Manchester, the big local clubs missed him, and he started his career with Crewe. In March 1967, Stoke City paid what in retrospect seems the laughably small sum of £19,500 for his transfer. He was capped in 1968 against England but, surprisingly, given the lack of Welsh inside-forwards, it was another five years before he won a regular place in the team. He seems, now, one of those Welshmen whose best is brought out when they play for their country. Joined Middlesbrough in 1977.

Sepp Maier (West Germany). This blond goalkeeper never plays better than on the great occasion, as he showed abundantly in such matches as the World Cup Finals game against Poland in Frankfurt in 1974, the World Cup Final itself against Holland in Munich, the European Cup Final the following year against Leeds United in Paris, for his club, Bayern Munich. On lesser days he has been known to look vulnerable on the crosses – one such moment even afflicted him when playing against Yugoslavia in the European Nations Cup semi-finals in Belgrade in June 1976 – but by and large he is a man for great occasions. He would probably have played in the World Cup Final of 1966 against England instead of Tilkowski, had he been fit. He did play for West Germany in the World Cup Finals of 1970 in Mexico, but was dropped for the third-place match after letting in four Italian goals in that extraordinary, unreal semi-final, when defences fell apart in extra time. He played in all three successful European Cup Finals for Bayern Munich between 1974 and 1976, for West Germany when they won the Nations Cup in Brussels in 1972. Born on 28 February 1944, he has now played over seventy games for West Germany.

Wilf Mannion (England). A blond inside-forward of great mobility and flair, a fine constructive player with the acceleration to go through and score goals himself, the war interfered with Mannion's still impressive career. Having won a place in the England team in the early 1940s, he later found himself serving with the Army in the Middle East. Born at South Bank, near Middlesbrough, he made his First Division debut for the local club at the age of seventeen, in 1937. The war over, he returned to them and to the England team, making in all twenty-six appearances, including the World Cup of 1950 in Brazil. He was one of the early footballing 'rebels', and was at one point suspended by the Football League for refusing to substantiate details of illegal payments which he'd allegedly received. But with Raich Carter (q.v.) and Jimmy Hagan he was the leading English inside-forward of his generation, confirming as much with a splendid display and two goals for Britain against the Rest of Europe at Hampden Park in May 1947.

Francisco Marinho (Brazil). A blond left-back who was one of the most exciting players of the 1974 World Cup, and certainly one of the few memorable players for Brazil. Tall, strong and fast, Marinho is the most eager and effective of overlappers, as England discovered to their cost in Los Angeles in May 1976 when he came on at half-time, transformed the game, and set up Brazil's winning goal. He has also, as he showed in the 1974 World Cup, a fulminating, left-footed dead-ball kick. Born on 8 February 1952 in the north of Brazil at Natal, he began with the local ABC club, then went to Nautico of Recife where the manager, Gradim, encouraged him to practise his free kicks. Botafogo brought him to Rio in late 1972, and he was an instant success. It looked as if Schalke 04 of Gelsenkirchen would bring him into the Bundesliga, but although he actually came there in 1975, he did not sign, returning to Botafogo; and their relieved supporters. He later joined Fluminense.

Marian Masny (Czechoslovakia). With the European Nations Cup Final of June 1976 in Belgrade, Masny won his twenty-second cap for Czechoslovakia and with it a victor's medal. Few deserved it more. His splendid, enterprising, incisive right wing play – not to mention his successful wanderings elsewhere – had played a great part in the Czechs' success. In the Final, it was he who had robbed Vogts on the right and paved the way to the first goal; even if, bursting through with characteristic acceleration, he had missed the chance later to make it 3–0. It was he who had left Gillard floundering on his home ground in Bratislava the previous

October, to cross for Gallis's winning goal against England. Born on 13 August 1950, a leading member of the Slovan team which dominated the Czech League in the mid-1970s, Masny has all the traditional Czech qualities of technique and poise, together with the pace they traditionally lacked; and a splendid swerve outside the back.

Josef Masopust (Czechoslovakia). European Footballer of the Year for 1962, it was Masopust, from his customary position of left-half, who opened the score for the Czechs in that year's World Cup Final in Santiago against Brazil. What a beautifully judged and taken goal it was! Masopust moved perfectly to the through ball from Scherer, deep and diagonal from the right, and shot impeccably wide of Gilmar in the Brazilian goal. The illusion was not to last, but the memory of the goal survives. Masopust was born on 9 February 1931, in Most, Northern Bohemia, and was taught football by his father, a miner. He played for the local teams, joined Teplice in 1948, and Dukla, the Army side which then swallowed up most of Czechoslovakia's best talent, in 1951; it then called itself UDA. Masopust was then an inside-forward, but the years saw him drop back to wing-half; the creative and adventurous member of a notable partnership with the solid Pluskal for club and country. A major in the Czech Army when at the peak of his football career, his other interests embraced jazz, comedians . . . and historical novels, up to the reign of Louis XIV. He followed his notable Czech career with a brief spell in Belgium.

Alex Massie (Scotland). Best known perhaps as a flawless right-half, a splendid user of the ball, Massie was also, however, an accomplished inside-forward. Though Hearts of Edinburgh were the club with which he made his name, and played for six distinguished years, he was actually born in Glasgow, playing for Shawfield Juniors and Glasgow Benburb, before joining Ayr United. When Aston Villa were desperately trying to fend off relegation in 1936, they signed Massie for a £6,000 fee. He won sixteen caps for Scotland, the first in season 1931–2 with Hearts, the last in 1937–8, with Villa. Massie stroked his passes for Villa with the same immaculate precision as he had for Hearts, and he himself later said he thought the 1937–8 Villa team which gained promotion from the Second Division was still better than the famous Hearts team for whom he had previously played. He eventually became team-manager of Aston Villa.

Stanley Matthews (England). The most legendary outside-right in the history of British football, Matthews's career in first class football lasted till he was fifty. Often despised and rejected by an England team for whom he gave such jewelled performances, passed over at times even by Stoke City, his first and last club, Matthews was living testimony to the English mistrust of brilliance. He was fully forty-one years old when, on the last of his many, distinguished returns to the England team, he played against Brazil at Wembley, turned Nilton Santos, that formidable left-back, inside out, and enabled England to score four goals which should have been six or seven. No one gave Santos such trouble in Brazil's winning World Cups of 1958 and 1962.

Born in the Potteries at Hanley on 1 February 1915, Matthews joined Stoke straight from school as the office boy, and was in their League team at seventeen, England's at nineteen. There, he began badly, with a muted debut against Wales, an uneasy second appearance in the notorious Battle of Highbury against Italy, after which Geoffrey Simpson, columnist of the *Daily Mail*, wrote that he had shown 'the same faults of slowness and hesitation' he had displayed against Wales, and suggested that he might not have 'the big match temperament'. Words that pursued him down the years.

For Matthews was nothing if not a great occasion player; indeed, the greater the occasion the more formidable he became. There is scarcely space to chronicle his exploits, but a few will suffice. The 1953 Matthews Cup Final, of course, when at long last, in his third Cup Final, he achieved a winner's medal, turning the depleted Bolton defence inside out and making the winner finally for Perry. That was with Blackpool, whom he'd played for as a guest throughout the war and joined after it for a mere £11,500. Then Blackpool made a generous gesture, selling him back to Stoke in 1961 for a token £2,500, Matthews promptly helping his original club back into the First Division.

Against Czechoslovakia at Tottenham in 1938 he switched to inside-right when a colleague was injured and scored three goals with his *left* foot to win England the game, 5–4. Earlier that year he had routed the German left-back Muenzenberg (sweet revenge for a poor performance against him in 1935) and England won, 5–4. In 1947 his brilliance helped England beat Portugal 10–0 in Lisbon, while the following year he ridiculed poor Eliani when England beat Italy 4–0 in Turin.

A slight, spare figure, Matthews relied on sheer talent; and a remarkable burst of speed once a full-back had been passed. His balance was exquisite, his willowy swerve, putting the full-back on the wrong foot before swaying by him on the outside, unmatched till the times of Finney and Garrincha. He was the son of Jack Matthews, The Fighting Barber of Hanley, while his own son, Stanley Junior, became a well-known tennis player.

For years, he'd put 10,000 on the gate whenever he played in London. In Europe, he was known as 'The Sorcerer'.

Ladislao Mazurkiewicz (Uruguay). Despite his Polish name and ancestry, Mazurkiewicz, one of the best goalkeepers of his epoch, a star of three World Cups, was dubiously recognized as a Spanish national and allowed to keep goal briefly for Granada, before packing up injured and going home to Montevideo, halfway through the 1975-6 season. His acrobatic excellence greatly helped Uruguay to reach the quarter-finals of the 1966 World Cup in England, the semi-finals in Mexico four years later, where he made a memorable save from Pelé, after clearing the ball straight to him. Not even Mazurkiewicz, however, could carry Uruguay's feeble, ill-tempered team in the German World Cup of 1974. Initially he was a full-back with the Racing Club, but he established himself as a goalkeeper with Penarol of Montevideo, helping them to win the Libertadores, South American, Cup in 1965 and 1966, the Intercontinental Cup against Real Madrid, without conceding a goal, the latter year. In November 1968, he kept goal in the second half in Rio for the Rest of the World against Brazil. Three years later, Penarol reluctantly transferred him, needing the fee, to Atletico Mineiro of Belo Horizonte, Brazil. Born 14 February 1945.

Sandro Mazzola (Italy). It is very rare that a son equals, even perhaps surpasses, his famous father at soccer, but Sandrino Mazzola has proved himself in every way but physically the equal of his late father, Valentino (q.v.), killed in the 1949 Superga air crash. Sandrino was only six years old then, and he and his family had to suffer privation in the years ahead, but Internazionale of Milan signed him, he came up quickly through their boys' team, and made his League debut in curious circumstances in 1961. Inter, as a protest, put out their complete youth team against Juventus, who thrashed it 9-1; but Sandro got the goal. Born in Turin on 8 November 1942, he made but a single further appearance the next season, but in 1962-3 won a regular place, scoring ten goals in twenty-three games; a centre-forward who made up for his flimsy physique with extreme quickness of thought and movement, and admirable ball control. He helped Inter to win two European Cups, in 1964 and 1965, followed by two Intercontinental titles, and made the first of his seventy appearances for Italy in May 1963 against Brazil, scoring from a penalty. He has figured in three World Cups, playing every game in 1966, running an odd 'relay' with Rivera, eternal Milanese rival (q.v.) in Mexico in 1970, playing again in Germany in 1974. His performances in the 1970 Final against Brazil and in the Stuttgart game of 1974 against Argentina were models of high morale and immense virtuosity. By this time he had become a creative inside-forward rather than a striker, a role he first successfully filled for Italy in the replayed Nations Cup Final against Yugoslavia in Rome in June 1968. A sensitive, fluent, intelligent man of firm character and opinions. Retired in 1977.

Valentino Mazzola (Italy). An inside-left of strength, skill and stamina, famous for the inside-forward partnership which he established with Loik for Venezia, and consolidated in the Torino and Italian national teams, both of which he captained. Torino, indeed, were about to win their fifth successive Championship when the plane carrying the team back from Portugal in May 1949 crashed on the hillside at Superga outside Turin, killing everyone in the party. Mazzola at that point had made a dozen appearances for Italy, the first on 5 April 1942 in Genoa against Croatia – that short-lived team – scoring in all four goals. He was then still playing for Venice, though actually he was born, on 26 January 1919, in the province of Milan at Cassano d'Ada. The leading Milanese clubs missed him, for he went from the local team to Alfa Romeo, and in 1939–40 to Venice, who sold him to Torino in 1942–3.

Giuseppe Meazza (Italy). Inside-right for Italy in their World Cup winning teams of both 1934 and 1938 – only Giovanni Ferrari, the inside-left, shared the distinction of figuring in each team – Meazza was in fact best known as a brilliant and prolific centre-forward, a master of technique, fifty-three times capped for Italy, scorer of thirty-three goals. He made his international debut on 9 February 1930, against Switzerland in Milan, scoring two goals for good measure. His last game, nine years later in Helsinki, was as inside-left and captain, against Finland. His whole international career was spent with Internazionale of Milan – known by Fascist decree as Ambrosiana-Inter, between the wars. Actually born in Milan on 23 August 1910, he made light of an indifferent physique, being wonderfully adroit on the ground, a most accurate shot, surprisingly good in the air. In all he scored 355 goals in first class football, having later spells with Milan, Juventus and Varese, returning to Inter as manager in 1946–7, and on one occasion resuming his boots and scoring twice for them. Later he would coach their junior teams.

Joe Mercer (England). Son of a former Nottingham Forest professional, Mercer was born in Ellesmere Port, Cheshire, and played in the county schoolboy team with two other famous England half-backs of the future, Stan Cullis (q.v.) and Frank Soo. In 1931, at the age of sixteen, he left the local club for Everton, where he became a spectacular attacking wing-half, excellent on either flank, though naturally left-footed, winning an England place in 1938–9, as did his club colleague Tommy Lawton (q.v.). The war saw both of them in the Army Physical Training corps and 'guesting' for Aldershot; members, too, of the very powerful Army representative team. In 1946 he had a bad knee injury, Everton proved unsympathetic, and were glad to sell him to Arsenal in November for a mere £6,500. Mercer's recovery was astonishing. Somewhat muting his game, a second stopper now rather than an attacker, but a splendid strategist, he inspired Arsenal to climb clear from relegation, win the League the following season, the Cup in 1950, the League again in 1953, before a leg broken against Liverpool at

Highbury put him out of the game the following year, with five full caps, three Victory caps and many wartime honours to his name. He briefly went into his father-in-law's grocery business, then became a manager with Sheffield United, Aston Villa and, after a breakdown in health, Manchester City; perhaps his best managerial period. In 1974, he also briefly took over the England team.

Billy Meredith (Wales). With Stanley Matthews (q.v.), the most celebrated and enduring outside-right in the history of British football. When he played his last match, for Manchester City, on 21 April 1925, he was fifty years old. His illustrious career began in the little North Wales village of Chirk, where the local schoolmaster, T. E. Thomas, Treasurer of the Welsh FA, was his mentor. From Chirk he went to Northwich Victoria, where he was considered 'slow' (it was once said of Matthews, too!); next to Manchester City, as an amateur. There he turned professional and his great gifts matured. His legs 'bony and bowed', as one writer put it, a toothpick forever in his mouth, he 'wriggled past opponents with a quick, elusive run' and either laid on splendidly accurate centres, or could score himself. His fifty-one matches for Wales stretched between 1894 and 1920, he scored the only goal of the 1904 Cup Final for Manchester City, he joined Manchester United in 1906 and added a Cup medal with them in 1909. He spent the last four years of his extraordinary career with Manchester City.

Jef Mermans (Belgium). One of the best of Belgium's centre-forwards, Mermans won fifty-six caps for his country. Splendid in the air, a powerful shot, quite Anderlecht's outstanding player until the arrival of Van Himst (q.v.). Josef Mermans, to give him his real name, was born in Antwerp, went to Brussels, and Anderlecht, for a record fee, and had few if any equals in Europe in the early 1950s. In fact he played inside-right for Belgium as early as 1945, and was actually on the right wing for Belgium in their two matches of the 1954 World Cup in Switzerland. At his best, however, Mermans, born in 1922, was the ideal centre-forward, not only a powerful attacker with two splendid feet, but also a player of unexpected grace notes, neat deviations with head or even heel, as capable of making openings for others as he was of firmly seizing them for himself. Many Italian clubs wanted him, but Anderlecht would not let him go.

Rajko Mitic (Yugoslavia). If Rajko Mitic hadn't struck his head on a girder in the dressing-room of the Maracana Stadium just before the vital 1950 World Cup match against Brazil, who knows how things might have been? His head had to be bandaged, he missed the opening minutes in which Brazil took the lead, and the Brazilians won the match 2–0. Mitic was an inside-right of all-round excellence, clever on the ball, a good distributor, a fine right-footed finisher, noted for his partnership at inside-forward with Boebk. He joined Red Star Belgrade in 1941 at the age of eighteen and played for them till he was thirty-six, winning fifty-nine caps, and figuring in the Olympic Cup Final of 1948 against Sweden at Wembley. In 1968 he was manager of the Yugoslav team which reached the Final of the 1968 Nations Cup in Rome, and, in the view of many, were cheated out of a merited success by some strange refereeing.

Luis Monti (Argentina and Italy). A fearsome figure of the 1920s and 1930s, Monti, a centre-half of the old, roving school nicknamed 'The Man Who Strolls', played for the Argentinian Olympic teams of the 1920s, joined Juventus of Turin in August 1931, played for Italy's World Cup winning team in Rome, three years later. A powerful, forceful player who could be described in somewhat less complimentary terms – the violent Argentinian footballer was not merely a phenomenon of the 1960s – Monti won the ball well, scored goals, gave the long, raking passes Vittorio Pozzo wanted when he managed the Italian national team. Born in 1901, Monti played for Boca Juniors and San Lorenzo de Almagro in Argentina, for whom he played in the World Cup Final of 1930 in Montevideo, won by Uruguay. When he got to Italy he was thirty years old, fat and out of condition, but he trained so hard that by 1932 he had won his place in the Italy team, gaining eighteen caps in all. It was his broken toe, suffered in the second minute of the England–Italy game of November 1934, that detonated the Battle of Highbury. Monti swore he had been kicked on purpose. The Italian players believed him and started kicking England with a vengeance. It should be said, however, that in Italy Monti became a dedicated, far more disciplined player.

Bobby Moore (England). Holder of the English record with 108 caps, Moore, always at left-half in international football, won the first of them at twenty-one in Lima against Peru in May 1962 on the way to the World Cup; in which he played every game. Four years later he captained England to World Cup success at Wembley and was named Player of the Tournament. In 1970, despite being arrested and detained in Bogota, Colombia, on trumped-up charges of stealing a bracelet in the Tequendama Hotel's Green Fire jewellery shop, he had another superb World Cup; perhaps even finer than in 1966. Ron Greenwood, Moore's mentor and manager at West Ham United, where he spent all but the last few years of his outstanding career, properly called him 'an occasions player'. The more important the match, the cooler and more resilient he seemed. He himself would say that he was a self-made rather than a natural player. A centre-half originally, tall, blond and very strong, he won a record number of youth international caps, and was renowned even then for his precociously cool demeanour. A superb reader of the game, a fine tackler, an expert calculator of how best he could use his own abilities, he captained West Ham to success in the Cup Final of 1964, the Cupwinners' Cup Final of 1965, again at Wembley, and was there again in the Fulham team beaten, ironically, by West Ham themselves, in 1975. Brought up in the East End of London, he joined West Ham straight from school, left for Fulham in 1974, had a spell with the San Antonio Thunder of the North American League in 1976. Of his many resilient international games, perhaps the best was against Brazil in the heat of Guadalajara at noon in the 1970 World Cup. Had Tostao not been allowed to push him off the ball before Brazil scored the only goal, who knows what the result might have been?

Stanley Mortensen (England). One of the finest opportunist, striking inside-forwards of the immediate post-war years, Mortensen was famous for his acceleration, his courage, his right-footed shot. In Italy he is still remembered for the amazing goal with which he opened England's score in Turin in May 1948; a shot almost from the goal line, on the right, which somehow found its way into the near, top corner. Signed by Blackpool from his native South Shields, he was originally considered slow, but determined speed work gave him the pace for which he was later celebrated; a lesson to those who lack it. He had bad head injuries when his bomber crashed on a training flight in the war, but with typical determination fought his way back, and first became prominent when playing as a guest for Bath City in wartime regional football. In 1944, when Ivor Powell was injured playing for Wales against England at Wembley, Mortensen was allowed to take his place as a substitute; his first international experience. In due course he would score 197 League goals for Blackpool and win twenty-five caps for England, including the World Cup of 1950 in Brazil. One of his best performances was against Sweden at Highbury in 1947 when he tipped the scales with a remakable hat-trick. He played for Blackpool in three Cup Finals, finishing on the winning side in the last of them in 1953, when he scored three of the four Blackpool goals. His partnership with Stanley Matthews (q.v.) was famous; in later years he had a short spell as manager of his old club.

Alan Morton (Scotland). Known as 'The Wee Blue Devil', an outstanding member of the Wembley Wizards who routed England at Wembley in 1928, Morton was a naturally right-footed outside-left who perfected his skills by kicking a tennis ball endlessly at a hole in a coal-shed wall, as a boy. 'Come away, the wee society man!' shouted a Rangers fan on one occasion, at Ibrox; a tribute to Morton's immaculate image off the field. On retirement he would become in 1933 a Rangers' director. His celebrated weaving and swerving were religiously practised twice a week. Born in Partick, he emerged with the Glasgow amateurs, Queens Park, and from there went to Rangers for whom he scored 115 goals in 495 games, playing thirty-one times for Scotland.

Gerd Muller (West Germany). Surely the most extraordinary goal-scoring centre-forward of all time, Muller got sixty-nine goals in sixty-two games for West Germany, at a time when defences had never been so well organized and tight, goals so hard to score. In May 1976 he took his total of Bundesliga goals for Bayern Munich to over 300; with a hat trick. He certainly has a proper sense of occasion, for his last goal for West Germany was that which won the 1974 World Cup Final; after which he announced that he would play no more international football, on the grounds that it was interfering with his family life. He continued, however, to play for Bayern, helping them to complete a hat trick of European Cup wins in 1975 and 1976. Squat, dark, very heavy in the thighs, Muller has tended to be underestimated throughout his career. He would have been turned down by Zlatko Cjaicowski (q.v.), then the manager of Bayern, had the club's President not overruled him; something of an inversion of the usual story. Muller then was playing for his local club at Noerdlingen, where he was born on 3 November 1945. He had already been turned down by two other clubs. Once with Bayern, however, his almost clairvoyant opportunism quickly established him as a remarkable player. It has been said of him that he 'only' scores goals; as if that were not the most difficult feat of all in this day and age. What goals they are! There was the delicate, looping deflection of the head with which he broke the Belgian resistance in the European Nations Cup semi-final of 1972, the left-footed volley with which he won the World Cup quarter-final at Leon against England in 1970, the second bite at the cherry with which he wheeled to get the winner against Holland in the 1974 World Cup Final; and so many, many more. He scored two glorious goals against Atletico Madrid in the replayed European Cup Final of 1974 in Brussels, another against Leeds in the Final of 1975 in Paris. No one has ever had quite his timing and menacing positional sense.

Johan Neeskens (Holland). Second only to Johan Cruyff among the outstanding figures of the brilliant Dutch team of the 1970s, Neeskens is a player who perfectly exemplifies Total Football. He has immense stamina, a strong tackle, great acceleration, a thundering right-footed shot. With this he scored five goals for Holland in the 1974 World Cup, three from the penalty spot, including one in the Final. But the most spectacular of all came in the rain at Dortmund, after an almost inconceivably fast break and exchange with Cruyff, a goal of devastating speed, simplicity and execution. He then joined Cruyff at Barcelona, to renew the partnership they had established with Ajax in Amsterdam. Born on 15 September 1951, Neeskens joined Ajax from Harlem, playing tennis, baseball and basketball – not to mention soccer as a goalkeeper – as well as football. He was at right-back when Ajax won their first European Cup Final at Wembley against Panathinaikos in May 1971, but then moved up to his true position in midfield. He had an excellent 1975–6 season with Barcelona, when Cruyff was inconsistent, but was sent off when he played his thirty-fourth game for Holland in Zagreb against Czechoslovakia in the Nations Cup semi-finals in June.

Igor Netto (Russia). A blond, attacking left-half who was one of the best individual Russian players to emerge during the 1950s, captaining the team which won the Olympic tournament in Melbourne in 1952, as well as his club, Spartak of Moscow. Altogether he won fifty-nine caps, but what should have been a successful World Cup tournament for him in Sweden in 1958 was ruined by a bad injury to his left knee; he played only once, at inside-left, in Gothenburg against Brazil, and was well below full prowess. In 1965 he came out of retirement to play at centre-half, and eventually became Sports Editor of Moscow Radio.

Gunter Netzer (West Germany). It was perhaps Netzer's misfortune that he should reach his remarkable peak as an inside-forward at the time of the 1972 Nations Cup finals, rather than two years later when the World Cup was played. In this, he got on the field only for a humiliating twenty minutes in the match at Hamburg against East Germany; Overath (q.v.) was preferred. There is little doubt, however, that the Beckenbauer–Netzer West German team of 1972 was more brilliant and spectacular, Netzer striding through defences with his flowing mane of blond hair, striking with those colossal size-eleven feet fifty-yard crossfield passes of astounding accuracy. It was that very stride which was perhaps his undoing, for it led to frequent pulled muscles. In

1973 he left the club with which he had grown up and whose team he'd inspired, Borussia Munchengladbach, for Real Madrid. Injury subverted him, though he had a better time of it when Paul Breitner (q.v.) arrived after the 1974 World Cup. In June 1976, Real Madrid released him, and he played for Grasshoppers (Zurich.) Born 14 September 1944.

Gunnar Nordahl (Sweden). Originally a fireman, and one of three brothers who figured in the excellent Swedish Olympic team which won the title in London in 1948, Gunnar Nordahl, a massive centre-forward, joined Milan that year and played for them with immense success. The trio of inside-forwards which he formed with his compatriots Gren and Liedholm (q.v.) was prolifically successful. The Championship was won in 1951, and again in 1955 when Nordahl, formidable in the air as on the ground, scored twenty-seven goals in his thirty-three games. Born on 9 October 1921 at Hornefors, he established himself with Norkopping, who dominated Swedish football in the late 1940s, and made a distinguished tour of England in 1946. Despite his bulk – he weighed towards the end of his career over 200 pounds – Nordahl was a deft, skilled player, not averse to dropping deep to create fresh problems for the opposing centre-half. First capped for Sweden in 1942, he scored the Rest of Europe's solitary goal against Britain at Hampden Park in May 1947, would have represented Sweden far more than thirty-three times had he not turned full pro with Milan, and scored no fewer than 225 League goals for the Italian club. In 1955 he moved south to Roma; and continued to score freely for several years.

Branko Oblak (Yugoslavia). A midfield player of great range who is just as happy to operate on either wing – as Wales found out to their cost in a Nations Cup match in Zagreb in April 1976 – Oblak has a wonderful left-footed shot, fine control, a capacity to strike a deadly through pass. One such brought Yugoslavia their spectacular opening goal against West Germany in Belgrade in the Nations Cup semifinal of June 1976. Born on 27 May 1947, Oblak won his forty-second cap that day, and another in the third place match against Holland. He played for Yugoslavia in the World Cup Finals of 1974, suffered a bad injury later that year, but in 1975 was fit and well enough to join Schalke 04 in the Bundesliga. In Yugoslavia his club was Hajduk of Split, with whom he won Championship honours. Joined Bayern Munich in 1977.

Ernst Ocwirk (Austria). Ocwirk was the last of the great attacking centre-halves of the Vienna School, both powerful and delicate, a big, dark player who made remarkable use of his left foot. Yet even he, by the World Cup of 1954, in which he helped Austria take third place, had become a proponent of the third-back game and was playing as an orthodox winghalf. Today he would have excelled as a midfield player. Born in Vienna on 10 March 1926, he made his international debut in 1947 and came to London the following year with the Austrian Olympic team. Fussball Klub Austria of Vienna were his team; he helped them beat Spurs at White Hart Lane just after Spurs had won the Championship in 1951, and later in the year hit the glorious long ball which enabled Ernst Melchior to score against England at Wembley. In 1956 he joined Sampdoria of Genoa in the Italian League, there becoming a successful, deep-lying inside-forward. On retirement he managed both F. K. Austria and Sampdoria.

Anton Ondrus (Czechoslovakia). Not many players have scored a dramatic goal for both sides in a major international tournament, but Ondrus did just that when playing for Czechoslovakia against Holland in the European Nations Cup semi-finals in Zagreb in June 1976. In the first half he went up to head a characteristic goal on the far post from a left-wing free kick; in the second half, a moment of distraction caused him to smash a right-wing centre off the crossbar and past his own astonished goalkeeper. All ended happily ever after. The Czechs won, and went on to prevail in the Final, where one of Ondrus's thundering breaks out of defence with the ball paved the way to their opening goal. He is a very tall, strong player, predictably dominant in the air, but surprisingly adroit on the ground. With Slovan Bratislava, he has won Championship honours and distinguished himself in the European Cup. Born 27 March 1950, the Nations Cup Final was his twenty-seventh international.

Vladimir Onishenko (Russia). Made his name as a fast, incisive, skilful left winger with Zaria Voroshilovgrad, the unfashionable team which surprisingly became Champions of Russia in 1972. In that year Onishenko played for Russia in the Final of the European Nations Cup against West Germany in Brussels, then went to Brazil to play in an international tournament for Russia; as represented by Zaria. Dynamo Kiev signed him despite the fact that they already possessed a famous left-sided player in Blokhin (q.v.) but the two hit it off splendidly both for club and country; as Onishenko's two excellent goals for Dynamo in the 1975 Cup Winners' Cup Final showed. Born 26 April 1949.

Raimondo Orsi (Argentina and Italy). Thirty-five games and thirteen goals for Italy was the impressive statistic of Orsi's second international career, the first having been achieved with his native Argentina. Distinguishing himself with them in the Olympiads of 1924 and 1928 as a spectacular left winger of great speed and glorious control, not to mention an excellent shot, Juventus brought Orsi to Turin for a huge salary and, after a brief period of 'quarantine', he did as well for them as he had in Buenos Aires. 1929 saw him win his first Italian cap; five years later it was his extraordinary, swerving, freakish shot – he couldn't repeat it the following day even with nobody in goal – that equalized for Italy in the World Cup Final against Czechoslovakia. Nicknamed 'Mummo', was born in 1901, the son of Italian immigrants.

Wolfgang Overath (West Germany). A major force in three West German World Cup teams, Overath at last won a medal in the Final of 1974 against Holland, having been on the losing side at Wembley in 1966. In 1970 his excellent performance and finely struck left-footed goal had given West Germany third place in Mexico City, but two years later Gunter Netzer (q.v.) had kept him out of the team that won the Nations Cup in Belgium. An excellent strategist, a splendid user of the long pass, but deft too with the short, diagonal ball, Overath was born on 29 September 1943, played for the local Siegburg 04 team, joined Cologne, whom he served so long and well, and made his debut for them at nineteen. By turns a schoolboy and youth international, he won his first full cap, one of eighty, against Sweden in November 1963. The last came in the 1974 World Cup Final, after which he announced his retirement from international football; a substantial loss to West Germany.

Carlo Parola (Italy). A tall, strong, polished centre-half famous for his overhead bicycle kick, Parola had some curiously unfortunate experiences on great occasions. Thus when picked as the only Italian to play for the Rest of Europe against Britain at Glasgow in May 1947, he put through his own goal. Three years later in Sao Paulo, a member of the Italian team defending the World Cup, he was run ragged by Sweden's Jeppson (q.v.). That was his last international cap, yet he was still only twenty-eight, having been born in Turin on 20 September 1920, playing for G. S. Fiat before joining Juventus at eighteen. In 1954 he was transferred to Lazio, but didn't last the season. Later he became a manager, with two periods at Juventus – the second a largely successful one, in which the Championship was won, ending in June 1976.

Pelé (Brazil). The finest player of his generation and perhaps the greatest of all time, Pelé won his first World Cup medal in 1958 at seventeen, his last in Mexico City in 1970, scoring in those two Cup Finals three spectacular goals, of which two were gloriously headed. In 1962, in Chile, injury had forced him to drop out of the eventually successful Brazilian team after a couple of games in Viña del Mar.

Born in October 1940, into a poor black family at Tres Coraçoes, in the huge state of Minas Gerais, he played at first for the little local club, Noroeste, but was a regular member of Santos's first team and a Brazilian international at the age of sixteen. Santos, whom he helped to win Brazilian and Intercontinental titles, were his only Brazilian club, though he came out of retirement in 1975 to join the New York Cosmos in a $4 million deal.

Standing only 5 foot 8 inches but weighing, in his prime, a muscular $10\frac{3}{4}$ stone, Pelé was – is – an extraordinary compound of animal grace, explosive reflexes, and subtle imagination. His balance is exceptional; allied to his strength, it allows him to ride the strongest of tackles. His fluid body swerves, his sleight of foot, enable him to beat opponents with apparent lack of effort. His heading power, his tremendous right-footed shot, have earned him well over 1,000 goals. In the 1970 World Cup, in Guadalajara, he once almost beat the Czech goalkeeper with a lob from the halfway line, and sold Uruguay's a dummy by placing the ball one side of him while running round the other!

Knocked down, he was up again like a rubber ball. Jumping, he could outleap the tallest defender, as he did to head Brazil's first goal in the 1970 World Cup Final. In the 1958 Final, his first goal, so cool as to make nonsense of his age, was scored when he caught the ball on his thigh, surrounded by defenders, hooked it over his head and volleyed it into the net.

A modest, disarmingly ingenuous, figure, Pelé could nevertheless look after himself. It was always his belief that a violent player must be paid in his own coin were he to be deterred. The coda of his career, in the United States, has been one of bland, patient diplomacy, occasional moments of amazing virtuosity. The Brazilians, who resented his refusal to play in the 1974 World Cup, resented his departure, too; but there's no doubt it was a boon to the growing game in North America.

Costa Pereira (Portugal). Goalkeepers, they say, mature late, and Costa Pereira, a tall, well-built, calm keeper, did not play for Portugal till he was thirty-one years old; in 1960–61 season. At once acrobatic and secure, Costa Pereira kept his place in the Portuguese team for years to come; including the 1966 World Cup when Portugal reached the semi-final and ultimately took third place. Meanwhile he was Benfica's goalkeeper in no fewer than four European Cup Finals, the first two of them – 1961 and 1962 – victorious. So might the fourth have been, in 1965, but he was hurt playing in driving rain against Inter in Milan, and beaten by a shot he might otherwise have saved, before having to give up his place in goal. By contrast it was his dramatic saves which kept the Cup for Benfica when they were such surprising winners over Barcelona in the 1961 Final in Berne. Born in Nacala, then Portuguese East Africa, Costa Pereira joined Benfica in 1954.

Luis Pereira (Brazil). Though sent off in the World Cup final rounds for a bad foul against Holland in Dortmund, Pereira was still one of the most imposing players of the competition; a black centre-half of great power, mobility and poise. Born at Juazeiro, Bahia, on 21 June 1949, his first major club was Salvador de Bahia, from whom he joined Palmeiras of Sao Paolo in 1968. There progress was barred by two excellent centre-backs, Nelson and Baldochi, and matters were complicated when Pereira was obliged to make his debut on his weaker, left, side. In due course, however, he established himself, and came to belie the nickname 'Chevrolet', given him for his impulsive dashes upfield. He still likes to take part in attacks, but he is much more judicious about it. In 1973 he established himself in the Brazilian national side with a series of excellent games on its European tour. In 1975 he was transferred at a huge fee to Atletico Madrid, together with his fellow Palmeiras player and Brazilian cap, Leivinha. Pereira adapted immediately, and was acknowledged one of the best defenders in the Spanish League when a knee injury towards the end of the season forced him to go back for an operation to Brazil.

Martin Peters (England). A hero of England's World Cup success in 1966, Martin Peters was a very latecomer to the team, having won his first cap, against Yugoslavia at Wembley, at right-half only the previous May. Nor did he play in the opening game of the World Cup tournament against Uruguay; but he took part in every one thereafter, functioning as a midfield player notionally deployed at outside-left. His great value to the team lay in his subtlety and his opportunism, these in turn supported by his immaculate technique. His was the cross which made the winning goal for his West Ham clubmate Hurst (q.v.) in the quarter-final against Argentina. He it was who banged in the second English goal in the Final against West Germany after Hurst's blocked shot had spun into the air. His right foot was always both powerful and very accurate; his ability to glide into striking positions unperceived exceptional. Moreover, he had great ability in the air. Born in the East End in Plaistow, so near to Upton Park, he went there from school, being by turn a schoolboy and a youth international. He was distressed when West Ham left him out of their 1964 Cup Final team, but was in the team which beat Munich 1860 the following year to take the Cupwinners' Cup, again at Wembley, and had his greatest satisfaction of all there in July 1966. In March 1970 he went to Tottenham Hotspur for a fee of £125,000 plus Jimmy Greaves, but his splendid partnership with Geoff Hurst – featuring those cunning crosses to the near post – was broken, and neither perhaps was ever quite the same player again. From Spurs he moved to Norwich City, and helped them to retain their First Division place in 1976–7.

Oswaldo Piazza (Argentina). Piazza's vibrant performance in the European Cup Final of May 1976 at Hampden was that of an old-fashioned, attacking centre-half, rather than a modern stopper. Perhaps one should simply say that it was a manifestation of Total Football at its most exciting. Piazza is a strongly built, very fast, extremely agile player with all the defensive qualities one would expect from an international centre-half, and formidable qualities when he goes forward. Born at Buenos Aires on 6 April 1947, he played for Argentina in the mini-World Cup, so-called, of summer 1972, then was persuaded to join Saint Etienne. He found adaptation very difficult, and was much hampered at first by linguistic difficulties, but once he had settled, he became an inspiration to the team, and one of the salient figures in their European Cup runs of 1973–5 and 1975–6. He made his name with Lanus of Buenos Aires.

Silvio Piola (Italy). The best centre-forward of the 1938 World Cup and one of the finest to emerge between the wars, Piola is somewhat wryly remembered in England for the goal he punched home against the English national team in Milan in May 1939; Dr Bauwens, the German referee, allowed it to stand. It was against England that Piola made his last, nostalgic appearance for Italy in May 1952 in Florence, at the age of thirty-eight; he was born at Robbio Lomellina on 29 September 1913. A further link with English football was forged when he became manager of the first Italian Under-23 team, which beat England 3–0 in Bologna early in 1954. Piola was tall, strong, no mean ball player, effective with foot and head. He and Meazza (q.v.) ran neck and neck for years as Italy's leading goal scorers, Piola finally prevailing, long after Meazza had retired, when he scored for Novara at Como in February 1951; which took his total to 356. He emerged with the once celebrated Pro Vercelli club in season 1929–30, joined Lazio of Rome in 1934, and is generally felt to have had his best years, eight of them, there, before going in turn to Turin, Juventus and Novara. His international debut was made in very demanding circumstances, in Vienna against Austria, the eternal rivals, on 24 March 1935. Italy won 2–0, Piola scored both goals. He played thirty-three internationals in all for a total of thirty goals, two of them coming in the 1938 World Cup Final against Hungary in Paris.

Pirri (Spain). Made his debut for Spain in demanding circumstances; against Argentina at Villa Park in the 1966 World Cup, heading the Spanish goal. He was then at right-half; in 1976 he was Real Madrid's sweeper, making frequent incursions up the field. A muscular, flexible player, Pirri – his real name Jose Martinez Sanchez – was born in Ceuta, North Africa, on 11 May 1945. After playing for four of the local teams he joined Granada as an amateur but moved to Real Madrid in 1963; still as an amateur to begin with. He got into the team initially as a 'deep' inside-forward, but was at right-half when they regained the European Cup in 1966. A footballer of great determination, technique and mobility, Pirri gave Spain and Real Madrid consistently excellent service for a decade.

Jan Pivarnik (Czechoslovakia). A blond right-back who overlaps splendidly, and who won his thirty-sixth cap for his country when the Czechs beat West Germany on penalties in Belgrade to take the 1976 European Nations Cup. Pivarnik is yet another Slovan Bratislava player, a full-back with the pace, dash and control of a winger, yet by no means lacking in defence. He was born on 13 November 1947. He originally played for VSS Kosice.

Frantisek Planicka (Czechoslovakia). This short, square, knee-padded figure was greatly admired in the 1934 World Cup, a goalkeeper sadly unlucky to be beaten by Orsi's freak equalizing shot in the Final in Rome. In 1938, Planicka was again captain and goalkeeper for the Czech World Cup team, and he continued to play occasional 'veteran' matches even into the 1970s! Born in 1904, he was capped seventy-four times, and made up for his lack of height with exceptional quickness and positional flair. His club was Slavia of Prague.

Carl Praest (Denmark). Rest of Europe outside-left for the May 1947 game in Glasgow against Britain, when he made the European goal by skilfully beating his man on the goal line more than once; then crossing for Gunnar Nordahl (q.v.) to score. The following year Praest was back again in Britain for the Olympic football tournament, this time playing as centre-forward in the Danish team which beat Britain 5–3 for third place. The year after that, and Praest had gone to Italy, to seek and make his fortune with the Juventus club of Turin, forming a celebrated left-wing partnership with his compatriot, John Hansen. Juventus promptly won the Championship, Praest missing only one game of the thirty-eight, and he added a further medal in 1952. Born in Copenhagen on 26 February 1922, he had the pace, control and shot of the classical W-formation winger.

Ferenc Puskas (Hungary). 'The Galloping Major', a reference to his rank in the Hungarian Army, may almost be said to have had two careers. The first ended with the Hungarian Revolution of 1956. Puskas, captain of a Hungarian team which had smashed England's unbeaten home record at Wembley in 1953 and just failed to win the World Cup Final of 1954 (when he was not really fit), found himself abroad with the Honved (Army) team. He stayed abroad, and after a period of suspension during which he lived in Milan, joined Real Madrid. There he managed to form a devastating partnership with the temperamental Alfredo Di Stefano (q.v.) who had previously brooked no rivals. In the 1960 European Cup Final at Hampden Park Puskas's unrivalled left foot scored four of Real's seven goals. In the 1962 Final in Amsterdam, he scored all Real's three goals, once running half the length of the field, and hitting another of his goals from a full thirty-five yards. His right foot was seldom evident, but it scarcely needed to be; seldom has a left foot of such power been seen in football. Born in Budapest in 1926 in the suburb of Kispest, developing with the Kispest club, he was first capped against Austria at the age of eighteen and scored one of Hungary's five goals. Altogether he scored eighty-five goals in eighty-four international games, and he also played for Spain in the 1962 World Cup in Chile. Stocky, even tubby, in build, his strength was complemented by pace off the mark and impeccable ball control; he could make goals just as brilliantly as he scored them. On retirement he became a coach, wandering the world, and taking Panathinaikos of Athens to the 1971 European Cup Final.

Jimmy Quinn (Scotland). A prodigious centre-forward who scored heavily for Celtic and Scotland in the early years of this century. In one especially memorable game between Scotland and England at Hampden Park, the Scots placed him at outside-left so he could be in direct opposition to

England's famous right-back Bob Crompton (q.v.). The exhibition of shoulder charging which ensued was robust and memorable. Quinn never gave any quarter, though as one Scottish official remarked, 'All the men Jimmy Quinn killed are living yet.' His nickname was 'Sunny Jim' or 'The Iron Man'. He was enormously strong, extremely brave, played for Celtic for twelve years from 1901 and gained eleven Scottish caps. He was a member of the first Celtic team to win the League and Cup double in season 1906–7.

Helmut Rahn (West Germany). An outside-right with the strength of a bull, great speed and a terrific right-footed shot, Rahn and his goals did as much as anyone or anything to win West Germany the 1954 World Cup; yet he was called up only at the last moment, when already on a South American tour with his team, Rot Weiss Essen. Born on 16 August 1929, he played forty times for Germany between 1951 and 1960, the first of his appearances in Istanbul against Turkey on 21 November 1951. He had a magnificent game in the 1954 World Cup Final in Berne against Hungary, scoring the equalizer after a corner, before half-time, and the winner when Fritz Walter's (q.v.) cross was pushed out to him. In the intervening years, a conviction for drunken driving seemed to menace his career, but Sepp Herberger, the little German team manager, had confidence in him, coaxed him back again, and he was as dangerous in the 1958 World Cup as he was in 1954. He scored four goals, including that which beat Yugoslavia 1–0 in the quarter-finals. In 1959 he was transferred to Cologne, but still kept his place in the West German team.

Alf Ramsey (England). Best known as the indispensable manager of England's 1966 World Cup winning team, Ramsey was a distinguished right-back in his time. Born in Dagenham in 1920, his early ambition was to become a successful grocer and he was a surprisingly late developer as a footballer. While on Army Service in the war in Hampshire, however, he began to play as an inside-forward for Southampton, with whom he eventually turned pro, dropping to full-back. In 1948 he won his first cap against Switzerland at Highbury, but then had the disconcerting experience of seeing Bill Ellerington take his place both with club and country. In the summer of 1949, however, he was transferred to Tottenham Hotspur for a large fee, and instantly established a rapport with the new manager, Arthur Rowe, the initiator of the 'push and run' game. Ramsey, never hurried, always constructive, a fine right-footed striker of the ball, was the perfect man to give the team poise and calm. It won the Second and First Division Championships in consecutive seasons, and Ramsey earned the nickname of 'The General'. He regained his place in the England team and went on to win thirty-two caps, three in the 1950 World Cup in Brazil, the last against Hungary at Wembley in November 1953. Then, as in the preceding game against FIFA, he scored coolly from the penalty spot; his free kicks were equally distinguished. On retirement he turned to management, brought Ipswich Town from the Third Division to the League Championship, took over England in 1962–3, instilled a new drive and morale, won the World Cup, and was ultimately replaced in April 1974.

Rob Rensenbrink (Holland). A left winger who, despite his success with the Dutch national team, has spent the best years of his career in club football with Bruges and Anderlecht, of Belgium. He is a forward of great quality, extremely fast, splendid on the ball, with the coolest of heads when an opportunity occurs; as West Ham found out in Brussels when he scored twice against them in the 1976 European Cupwinners' Cup Final for Anderlecht. Born at Oostzaan on 3 July 1947, he turned pro with DWS of Amsterdam, after amateur days with OSV. His career was then pursued in Belgium. He made his international debut on 30 May 1968, against Scotland, and who knows what might have happened in the 1974 World Cup Final had he been fully fit, rather than forced to play with a pulled muscle, eventually being substituted? Rensenbrink was, however, fully fit in the European Nations Cup Finals of 1976 in Yugoslavia, where the third place match in Zagreb, won by Holland, brought him his twenty-seventh cap.

Luigi Riva (Italy). Gigi Riva was burdened by the immense weight of expectation put on him by the Italian public. Before the 1970 World Cup, in particular, one almost had the impression he was expected to win it on his own. In the event, he did not really come to life until the quarter-finals, with two splendid goals against Mexico, to which he added a memorable third when he scored against West Germany from outside the box in the semi-final. Riva's career has not been lucky or easy. He broke his left leg in 1967, his right leg in 1970, and had the courage to come back as effectively as ever each time. He was ignored inexplicably for the 1966 World Cup, in which Italy were humiliated by North Korea. He was ignored as a youngster by the great northern clubs, and had to sign for Legnano of the Third (C) Division, for whom he made his debut in 1962–3. The following season he joined Cagliari, then still an obscure Sardinian club in Serie B, the Second Division. Riva's eight goals in twenty-six games in his first season took them into Serie A where they have stayed, actually winning the title in 1970, with Riva scoring twenty-one goals in twenty-eight games. His qualities as a striker have been pace, courage, enterprise and a searing left-footed shot. Though he began as a left winger, he has always liked to play both centre *and* left. Italy first capped him in June 1965. In the summer of 1973 he could have been transferred to Juventus for the equivalent of £1½ million, but angrily refused. In 1974 he played again in the World Cup, but so unsuccessfully that he was dropped from Italy's last game. For all that he has been the most admired and incisive Italian forward since the war. He was born at Leggiuno on 7 November 1944.

Roberto Rivelino (Brazil). Rivelino's enormously powerful left-footed shooting, both from free kicks and in open play, was a feature of Brazil's World Cup victory in Mexico in 1970. In 1974, when in West Germany he found the burden in midfield rather too much for him, his free kicks were Brazil's chief hope of goals, but by 1976, he was showing constructive qualities to match his scoring powers. He had, after all, first emerged as an inside-forward considered a challenger to the equally left-footed Gerson (q.v.). The problem was, fitting them both into the team, but Zagalo (q.v.), Brazil's manager in 1970, solved it neatly by using Rivelino as a deep-lying left winger. A somewhat bandit-like figure, with his abundant moustache, long hair, thick thighs, Rivelino was born in Sao Paolo on 19 January 1946, and emerged with the local club, the Corinthians. He made his debut for Brazil against Mexico in 1968, but at that time it was feared that he lacked the stamina for a full game in midfield. He scored three times for Brazil in the 1970 World Cup, besides putting over the cross from which Pelé headed the first goal of the Final. In the 1974 tournament he added another three goals, two of them in the semi-final group, a clever free kick to beat East Germany, a typical swerving shot to score against Argentina. Two years later, though some of his pace might have gone, his short and long ball distribution was wonderfully quick and precise. By then he was with Fluminense of Rio.

Gianni Rivera (Italy). A First Division player at fifteen with Alessandria, transferred to Milan for a huge fee at sixteen,

Gianni Rivera has always been 'The Golden Boy' of Italian football. It was scarcely even a surprise when, in 1975-6, he actually confronted the President of Milan, Buticchi, in a battle over the control of the club, and forced him to sell his shares, thus gaining the control of the club. The son of an Alessandria railwayman who moved with him to Milan, Rivera played for the Italian Olympic team in 1960 on the right wing before he was seventeen, but subsequently moved to his proper position of creative inside-forward. Though apparently fragile, his technique and timing enable him to hit long passes as well as short, and to strike some remarkable long range goals. He evades tackles beautifully, and can score when it matters; as he did against Mexico in the quarter-finals of the 1970 World Cup, and again in the semi-finals against West Germany, when his was the winning goal. The Final was less happy for him, since he was brought on as a 'diplomatic' substitute a mere and farcical six minutes from the end. As for the 1974 World Cup, it ended sadly for him, since he was dropped after a poor performance in Stuttgart against Argentina. 1966 was little happier; he played two games in England, the second being the North Korean defeat at Middlesbrough. Born on 8 August 1943, Rivera has been a controversial as well as a celebrated player in Italy; there have been those who found him too peripheral to the action, though his record is surely self-explanatory. For Milan he has won not only Championship medals but honours in the European, the Cupwinners' and the Intercontinental Cup. For Italy he played sixty games and scored fourteen goals. Given the bruising exigencies of the Italian Championship, the pressures of international football, it is surely a career to admire.

Charlie Roberts (England). One of the best attacking centre-halves in British football prior to the Great War, Charlie Roberts would have won many more than three caps had he not been an intransigent founder of the Players' Union, and had brushes with officials of the Football League. It was also suggested that Roberts's 'rudeness' to F. J. Wall, the authoritarian Secretary of the Football Association, was at the bottom of his exclusion from England teams: an event which supposedly took place in the dressing-room just after Roberts and Manchester United had won the 1909 Cup Final. Vittorio Pozzo, team manager of Italy's 1934 and 1938 World Cup winning teams, admired him so much when he was a student in England that he sought his advice, in long conversations, and modelled his teams on Roberts and his play. Roberts was tall, strong, exact, a fine user of the long pass which Pozzo so admired.

Pedro Rocha (Uruguay). A tall, dominant, creative inside-forward who played in four World Cups, from 1962 to 1974, Rocha's injury at the beginning of the 1970 tournament in Mexico greatly affected Uruguay's challenge; even though they reached the semi-final. For they had relied on Rocha for many years to bind the team together and set up its chances. He was only nineteen when he played in the 1962 tournament. Penarol was his Montevidean club, and in 1966 he helped them to add the Intercontinental title to the South American Libertadores Cup. He was transferred in 1970 to Sao Paolo of Brazil.

Dominique Rocheteau (France). One of the most exciting players to emerge in France for many years, Rocheteau's dashing play on the right wing, his speed, skill and enterprise, had much to do with Saint Etienne's passage to the 1976 European Cup Final at Hampden Park. They might even have won it had he been able to play the whole game, rather than come on only in the concluding minutes, owing to injury. Even then he had time to make his presence felt, his electric runs alarming the Bayern Munich defence, his close control causing them vast difficulty. Rocheteau, curiously enough, was the stone that the builder rejected. As a youth in 1969–70, he reached the final of an international competition for skills, in Paris. He came last of twenty-two, and was ignored by every club save Saint Etienne, whose famous scout, Pierre Garonnaire, liked what he saw. The problem then was to convince Rocheteau's father, whose family had for generations raised and sold oysters, that professional football was a proper occupation for his son. Dominique preferred physical education to oysters in any case, and he was allowed to join Saint Etienne. In 1973–4 a bad injury to his right knee threatened his career, but he eventually surmounted this. He was born on 14 January 1955, at Saintes, and established himself in the French international team solidly in 1975–6.

Leigh Richmond Roose (Wales). A notable if somewhat eccentric goalkeeper, one of the best ever to play for Wales, whom he represented on a dozen occasions. Starting with Aberystwyth, playing then for the now defunct London Welsh, he continued his career with Stoke, Everton, Stoke again and Sunderland. Medicine was his profession, football his diversion, practical joking his penchant. Ivan Sharpe, an amateur international himself and a leading journalist in his day, called Roose 'the most discussed goalkeeper of all time,' and recalled a game he played with him for Northern Nomads when 'it was not easy to discover whether he was goalkeeper or full-back.' For all that, Roose's distinguished international career stretched from 1900 to 1907.

Djalma Santos (Brazil). A massively built black right-back who overlapped, as Brazilian full-backs love to do, and played in both the 1958 and the 1962 World Cup Finals. The 1958 Final was in fact his first game in those Swedish matches, the place having been previously filled by De Sordi.

But Santos gave an immaculate performance, completely playing the dangerous Skoglund (q.v.) out of the game. In 1962 he was responsible for provoking the third Brazilian goal in the Final in Santiago when he turned back almost casually to boot a prodigious left-footed centre into the sun. Schroiff the Czech goalkeeper dropped it, Vavà scored. Born in Sao Paulo in 1929, he began his career with the Portuguesa club, was transferred from there to Palmeiras, and played his first World Cup in Switzerland in 1954, when he was not altogether peripheral to the infamous Battle of Berne, against Hungary. His last World Cup was rather a sad anticlimax, for he played two games for Brazil in England in 1966, but at Everton found the pace and flair of the Hungarians too much for him, at the age of thirty-seven.

Nilton Santos (Brazil). Played most successfully for Brazil in the 1962 World Cup Final in Santiago against the Czechs at the age of thirty-six. Four years earlier he had almost casually snuffed out the threat of Sweden's Kurre Hamrin (q.v.) in the World Cup Final in Stockholm. Composure was the essence of this tall, strong, polished left-back's game, and he was always eager to come forward, scoring many a goal with his strong left-footed shot. At twenty-three he played for Brazil in the 1949 South American Championships, but was only a reserve for the 1950 World Cup, which was held in Brazil. By 1954 he was a regular member of the team, but was sent off against Hungary in Berne after coming to blows with Josef Bozsik (q.v.). Born at Ilha do Governador, he made his name with Botafogo of Rio, and went on playing for Brazil till he was forty, winning more than eighty caps.

Dr Gyorgy Sarosi (Hungary). A leading Hungarian footballer of the 1930s, a successful manager in Italy in the 1950s when he won the 1951–2 Championship with Juventus, Dr Sarosi was both a splendid attacking centre-half and a dangerously incisive centre-forward. The latter was the position he filled in the 1934 and 1938 World Cups. He captained Hungary to the 1938 Final, in which he scored one of their two goals against the victorious Italians. His career was spent with the Ferencvaros club of Budapest, and he scored forty-two goals in sixty-six games for his country, including five in a 5–3 win against Austria in 1936, seven out of eight the following year against Czechoslovakia. A first class fencer, swimmer and tennis player, he also had a Ph.D in law. A polymath indeed.

Juan Schiaffino (Uruguay and Italy). Born in Montevideo on 28 July 1925, Schiaffino was a remarkable inside-left, tall, pale and apparently frail, but a glorious ball player who could swerve and dribble his way out of the tightest corner, a magnificent passer of the ball – not least the defence-splitting through pass – and sometimes a decisive goal scorer. He never got a more important goal than the equalizer against Brazil in the decisive World Cup match of 1950 in the Maracana Stadium, striking home Ghiggia's pass. Four years later, in Switzerland, he looked just as effective when forced to play most of the quarter-final game against England at left-half, owing to injuries to other players. He was a member of the all-amateur Uruguayan team which, thanks to a strike of professionals, contested the 1949 South American Championship; the following year found him helping them to win the World Cup. In 1954 Milan bought him and scarcely had he arrived in Italy when the fatuously permissive Italian rules enabled him to play for Italy against Argentina. He might even have played for Italy in a World Cup, but Northern Ireland, in 1958, knocked them out. Schiaffino, whose Uruguayan football was played with Penarol, finished his career in Italy with Roma, then went back to become both a club and, in 1975, the international team manager.

Elisha Scott (Ireland). Scott was the last manager of Belfast Celtic, the club which died in 1949 and with whom he concluded his playing career and won his last international caps, in 1936. Thirty-one times capped for his country, his splendid international career stretched over sixteen years, his first cap being won in season 1919–20. Always safe, never showy or spectacular, he saved Ireland on many occasions against stronger opposition. In his distinguished twenty-two years with Liverpool, he won Championship medals in 1922 and 1923. It is of him that the apocryphal story is told; that meeting 'Dixie' Dean (q.v.) of Everton on Liverpool Station, Dean nodded a greeting and Scott, through sheer force of habit, threw himself full length on the platform!

Uwe Seeler (West Germany). 'Uwe, Uwe!' cried the German fans, as a battle cry, and before the era of Franz Beckenbauer, no player more perfectly embodied the ethos and force of West German football. Seeler played with success in no fewer than four World Cups even though, by an irony, he was never on the winning side in any of them. Not tall but most solidly built, and a magnificent jumper (recall his back-headed, 'impossible', goal against England in the 1970 World Cup quarter-finals in Leon), Seeler was born in Hamburg, and played his first international at the age of seventeen when he came on as substitute against France on 16 October 1954. Germany lost 3–1, as they did when Seeler, now eighteen, played on 1 December in the next match against England at Wembley. By 1958 he was a confident international, though his World Cup debut against Argentina in Malmo that June, when he scored, was surprisingly enough his first cap since March 1956. He scored again against Northern Ireland, and made the left-wing cross from which Hans Schaefer volleyed a superb goal against Sweden in the Gothenburg semi-final. In 1960 he helped Hamburg win the German Championship, after which they had a good European Cup run. In Chile in 1962 he scored against the Swiss, dived to head a typically unexpected, courageous goal against Chile themselves; and West Germany reached the quarter-final. Not even an operation to fit an artificial Achilles tendon could deter him; or prevent him jumping as high as ever. He was a star of the West German team which got to the World Cup Final of 1966 against England, and a dynamic inside-right in Mexico in 1970. There Helmut Schoen, the manager, lined him up beside the new star Gerd Muller (q.v.) who would eventually beat his scoring record; and with great success. They combined to work out a memorable headed goal in the semi-finals, when West Germany were unlucky to lose to Italy. The World Cup over, Seeler announced his retirement from international football, a course emulated by Muller four years later, but he continued for a while to play for Hamburg.

Dragoslav Sekularac (Yugoslavia). A controversial but exceptionally talented inside-forward of gypsy origin, dark, small, sturdily built, an inside-forward with vision, control and a fine shot, Sekularac was twice given eighteen-month suspensions for indiscipline by the Yugoslav Federation. For all that he was their star player of the 1962 World Cup, when they got to the semi-final in Chile, binding the team together. He was only twenty when he played his first World Cup in Sweden in 1958, having emerged with the famous Red Star team of Belgrade. The 1970s found him playing football in Colombia, a wanderer to the last, still able, however, to beat his man in that casual, jinking way which implied that it was a tiresome necessity.

Len Shackleton (England). Shackleton entitled his autobiography *Clown Prince of Soccer*, and devoted a chapter of one blank page to 'The Average Director's Knowledge of Soccer'. In 1976, he himself became a director of Fulham. There's an analogy with Charlie Buchan. Both began as amateur inside-forwards with the Arsenal and left them, both played far less often for England than their talents merited, on the grounds that they were too idiosyncratic for the others to fit in with them. Shackleton in 1939 went back to his native Bradford, joined the local Park Avenue club, and worked through the war in the mines. Arsenal had found him too frail, but now he added sufficient strength to his extraordinary gifts; arms delicately held akimbo, he picked his way tantalizingly past defenders, and made jewelled passes to his fellow attackers. Newcastle United bought him for over £13,000 in 1946, a year in which he had earlier played a Victory international for England at Hampden, but he was soon on the move again – to the rival North Eastern club, Sunderland, in 1948, for £20,500. He stayed with them for nine years, in the course of which he won but five England caps, giving a memorable display and scoring a brilliant goal against Germany at Wembley in December 1954; one of those rare days when England threw caution to the winds and picked a team of ball players.

Matthias Sindelar (Austria). Known for his spindly physique as 'Der Paperiener' ('The Man of Paper'), Sindelar was the elegant centre-forward of the Austrian Wunderteam of the early 1930s, a footballer of consummate accomplishment, able to weave his way through a defence as if by sorcery. He modelled himself on Kalman Konrad, a celebrated Hungarian attacker who played for his club, F. K. Austria, in the 1920s. Like Konrad he had a strong shot; but he preferred if he could to walk the ball into goal. He was outstanding when Austria frightened England at Stamford Bridge in 1932, played in the World Cup of 1934, but died a wretched death in Vienna early in the Second World War. He killed himself in a gas-filled room when a fellow member of the Wunderteam, an ardent Nazi, betrayed him to the Gestapo as being part Jewish.

Omar Sivori (Argentina and Italy). Yet another Argentinian co-opted by Italy on the strength of his ancestry, Sivori was a dazzling inside-left who came to fame in the South American Championships of 1957 in Lima, Peru. He was one of the so-called 'Trio de la Muerte' ('Trio of Death'), otherwise nicknamed 'The Angels With Dirty Faces', which brought Argentina the title. Maschio and Angelillo were the others; they, too, went to Italy. Sivori, indeed, went within a few months; to Juventus of Turin for £91,000. Small, dark, but beautifully balanced, infinitely elusive and a deadly left-footed shot, he had nearly a decade of success with Juventus before being transferred in 1965 to Naples. In 1973 he was a most successful team manager of Argentina, getting them to the Finals of the 1974 World Cup but, intransigent to the last, unable to suffer fools gladly on or off the field, he quarrelled with the Argentinian officials and departed before the Finals themselves. He played for Italy in Chile in the World Cup of 1962. Born in a suburb of Buenos Aires, San Nicolas de los Aroyos, on 2 October 1935.

'Nacka' Skoglund (Sweden). An inside- or outside-left with bright blond hair, Lennart ('Nacka') Skoglund joined AIK Stockholm from the local Hammarby club in 1949, when still nineteen – he was born in Stockholm on 24 December 1929 – and within a year was a world star. The World Cup of 1950 was the stage on which he established himself, his precocious skills at inside-forward – where he teamed so well with Palmer – helping Sweden to knock out Italy and ultimately take third place. Internazionale swooped and brought him to Milan. There he was an instant success, delighting the crowds with the boyish insouciance of his play. He helped them win the Championship in 1952–3, and again in 1953–4, when he moved on to the left wing and was able to give his natural, attacking tendencies full rein. In 1958, when Sweden at long last introduced full professionalism, he was able to return to their team, after eight years' absence, to play in the World Cup in his native country. His speed, skill and left-footed shot helped Sweden to reach the Final. Marrying an Italian girl, he eventually left Inter for Sampdoria of Genoa, returned to Sweden, and died in Stockholm, still pitifully young. His two sons, however, both became professional footballers, the younger of them signing for Inter in July 1976.

G. O. Smith (England). Noblest Corinthian among English centre-forwards, and still estimated one of the best, despite his reluctance to head the ball, G. O. Smith learned his football at Charterhouse School, played soccer and cricket for Oxford University, then led the attack of the Corinthians. 'If forwards have to head, there was something wrong with the side,' was his view. He played twenty-one times for England between 1893 and 1901, famous for his crisp shooting, his passes to the wings, and he would have won more caps had not the death of another distinguished player, Arthur Dunn, Headmaster of Ludgrove preparatory school, forced Smith to devote more time to teaching. His first game was against Ireland in Birmingham, his last, when he captained England and scored twice, against Germany in 1901 at Tottenham; an all-amateur English team won 12–0. He was born at Croydon on 25 November 1872, and died after a stroke in 1943, most gentlemanly of great footballers.

Billy Steel (Scotland). Living now in Los Angeles, Billy Steel became an international star in his very first match for Scotland; against England at Wembley in April 1947. The Scots were expected to be thrashed, but the ebullience of Steel, a small, blond figure, full of dash and pace, not to mention ideas, with a splendid shot, galvanized his team. They drew 1–1 and deserved to win. A few weeks later, to the general surprise, Steel was preferred to such Titans as

Carter and Doherty (q.v.) at inside-left in the Great Britain team that played Europe at Hampden Park, in his native city. Nor did Steel disappoint the selectors, for he scored a spectacular goal from twenty-five yards. Transferred to Derby County in 1947 for a then record of £15,000, from his original club Morton, he stayed there for three years, an outstanding figure, then went to Dundee, where from 1950 to 1953 he retained his place in Scotland's team.

Clem Stephenson (England). Though he received but one international cap for England, against Wales in season 1923–4, Stephenson was perhaps the most admired inside-left of his era. 'A great schemer and tactician,' Charlie Buchan wrote of him, 'Clem brought the best out of his colleagues by his accurate, well-timed passes. He was by no means fast but he made the ball do the work.' It was Stephenson who told Buchan during the 1913 Cup Final, Aston Villa against Sunderland, that he had dreamed Villa would win 1–0 through a goal by Tom Barber. Sure enough Barber headed a freakish goal from an apparently badly directed corner; and Villa won. After the war Herbert Chapman signed him for Huddersfield Town where he made up a dazzling left wing with Billy Smith, which for unfathomable reasons the England selectors never chose. Stephenson was the captain and guiding force of the Huddersfield Town team which won three consecutive League titles between 1923 and 1925. He was a North Easterner, like so many great English footballers, born at Seaton Delaval.

Luis Suarez (Spain). Suarez's career in Italy was as exceptional as his career in Spain. He was unquestionably among the best European inside-forwards of the 1960s, a player of power, skill, stamina and vision who first inspired Barcelona then was the great midfield force in the Internazionale (Milan) teams that won European and Intercontinental

Cups. Born at Riazor, La Coruna, on 2 May 1935, his close control, swerve and originality led Barcelona to sign him when he was eighteen, and he won his first Spanish international cap in 1957. He helped Barcelona to reach the European Cup Final of 1961, and soon afterwards joined Inter for £210,000. The following year he played for Spain in the 1962 World Cup in Chile, but now his international appearances were sporadic. He did, however, represent the Italian League, and play for Inter in their victorious European Cup Finals of 1964 and 1965. On retirement, he stayed in Italy as a manager.

Wim Suurbier (Holland). Made up with Rudi Krol (q.v.) the splendid pair of attacking full-backs who were so successful both for Ajax and Holland. Suurbier, though known as a right-back, was actually at left-back, replacing the injured Krol, when Ajax first won the European Cup at Wembley against Panathinaikos of 1971, and at right-back, partnering Krol, when they retained it in 1972 and 1973. Like Krol he is mobile, quick, enterprising, and strong. Born at Eindhoven on 16 January 1945, he came to Ajax as a junior in 1963, turned professional a year later, won his first Dutch honour on 6 November 1966 against Czechoslovakia. When Holland won the third place Nations Cup match in Zagreb in June 1976, it was his forty-seventh appearance.

Frank Swift (England). A tall goalkeeper with huge hands and acrobatic agility, Frank Swift played at Wembley as a nineteen-year-old when he helped Manchester City win the 1934 Cup Final, but had to wait over nine years before he played there for England. Once he was in the England team he stayed there for the best part of nine years, his final appearance being made in Oslo against Norway in 1949. He fainted in that 1934 Cup Final when the photographers behind his goal counted off the minutes to the end. He and his brother, who kept goal for Blackpool – who also wanted Frank – ran a pleasure boat on Blackpool beach for a while. Frank got a job in the gasworks, played non-League football for Fleetwood, turned professional with Manchester City in October 1932, made his League debut for them at Derby on Christmas Day 1933. He was their first team goalkeeper thereafter, with very few exceptions. He was a great humourist in goal, an enormously popular figure, whether playing for City, England, the Army or Aldershot, with whom he appeared during the war as a guest. Winning nineteen full England caps – plus all those appearances in the war – he retired from the game in 1950, became a journalist, but alas died in the Munich air crash of February 1958, when travelling with the Manchester United team. He was then only forty-three.

Bobby Templeton (Scotland). 'This wonderful Association forward has been at once the delight and despair of countless thousands,' wrote Pickford and Gibson in *Association Football and The Men Who Made It* of Templeton, in 1906, when he was spending a brief period delighting the fans of Woolwich Arsenal. As his chroniclers suspected, however, he was not in South-East London for long, maintaining his reputation for persistent restlessness. An outside-left of marvellous gifts, tremendously fast and clever, he gained his eleven Scottish caps between 1902 and 1912 with Aston Villa, Newcastle, Woolwich Arsenal and Kilmarnock, and he was also a member of the famous Celtic forward-line early in the century. 'There is nothing of the steam-roller about his methods,' wrote the enraptured Pickford and Gibson, who extolled 'the wondrous versatility of the man . . . the grace and beauty of his movements'. Consistency is seldom to be found in such artists of the football field, and Templeton was no exception, but he was, at his best, quite clearly one of the great entertainers of his day.

Colin Todd (England). Though Colin Todd won his first England cap, against Northern Ireland at Wembley in May 1972, at right-back, and played there again with exuberance in the summer of 1976, he is best known as a defensive half-back, a second stopper of great speed, strength and versatility. He was petulantly suspended by England for refusing to make an Under-23 tour, but it was inevitable that when Bobby Moore dropped out of the team, the place should ultimately be Todd's; and so it was. Born in the North East at Chester-le-Street, he joined Sunderland from school, and played for them till 1970–71, when Derby County paid a large fee for him. He has so far helped them to win two Championships, and has excelled in the European Cup. A low centre of gravity increases Todd's mobility, and when he plays right-back, he appreciates the extra freedom to go forward in attack with the ball.

Tostao (Brazil). A wretched accident in training, when a ball hit him in the eye and detached a retina, blemished the career of this greatly gifted centre-forward. Operations in Houston, Texas, enabled him to play and win a medal in the 1970 World Cup, but the trouble recurred, and he had to retire before the 1974 competition. He had played at the age of nineteen in the 1966 World Cup and scored a fine goal against Hungary at Everton, though Brazil lost 3–1. His strong left foot, splendid balance, lively movement and technique were already in evidence, but by 1970 he was something more, a centre-forward who splendidly kept his line together, often playing brilliantly with his back to the goal, a master of flicks and deviations. He had already scored nine goals in the qualifying tournament, and he scored twice against Peru in the quarter-finals of the competition proper at Guadalajara. A student of economics in Belo Horizonte, he emerged there with the Cruzeiro club, but in 1973 came to Rio to play for Vasco da Gama; alas, so very briefly. His real name was Eduardo Conçalves de Andrade.

Bert Trautmann (Germany). Perhaps one should say England rather than Germany for although he is indeed a German, fought with the Nazi paratroops in the war in Russia, and was long after it detained in a Lancashire prisoner-of-war camp, Berg (to give him his correct name) Trautmann spent the whole of his professional footballing career in England. It must have seemed to Manchester City fans that there would never be 'another' Frank Swift, but the huge, blond, fearless, acrobatic Trautmann equalled and perhaps surpassed him. The greatest irony of all was that he wasn't qualified to play for England, while West Germany never capped him. At first he turned out for St Helen's in minor football, but Manchester City found him there and brought him to Maine Road. He helped them to win the 1956 Cup Final, and stayed on the field even though he actually broke his neck in a collision. Between 1951 and 1965 he played no fewer than 508 League games for City. Later, but not for very long, he managed Stockport County. Born in Bremen, he stood 6 feet $1\frac{1}{2}$ inches, and weighed over 13 stone.

Francois Van der Elst (Belgium). The versatility of Van der Elst is shown by the fact that he made his name and won his place in the Belgian international team as an outside-right, was notionally in midfield when he played so galvanically, and scored, against West Ham for Anderlecht in the 1976 Cupwinners' Cup Final in Brussels, but had previously played right-back during that competition. Essentially he *is* an outside-right, with the pace, control and penetration to breach defence and score goals, but, in the fashion of the times – and Total Football – he is happy to start his runs from as deep as midfield; or even right-back. Only twenty-one when he won his medal in the Cupwinners' Final, he is a player of dynamism and great potential.

Wim Van Hanegem (Holland). Van Hanegem has what one might call a surly brilliance, a big, heavy, strong inside-left with a magnificent left foot, splendid strategy – and little pace. That he nevertheless became one of the game's best midfield players, a star of the 1974 World Cup Final in Munich, testifies to the development of his other qualities. Born at Breskens on 20 February 1944, he began with the amateur club, Velox, then joined the once renowned Xerxes of Rotterdam. When they disintegrated he went, in 1968, to Feyenoord, and was an instant success, a goal scorer with left foot or head as well as an orchestrator. He played a major part in Feyenoord's success in the 1970 European Cup, not least in the Final against Celtic in Milan. First capped for Holland on 30 May 1966 against Scotland, he won his forty-sixth cap against Czechoslovakia in Zagreb ten years later; a match in which alas he was sent off the field for arguing. His free kicks, one should add, have always been enormously subtle, powerful and dangerous.

Paul Van Himst (Belgium). Born on 2 October 1943, Van Himst has been that rare phenomenon, the boy wonder who achieved a long career. He was only seventeen when he was first chosen Belgium's Footballer of the Year, as a centre-forward of poise and penetration; at eighteen, he won the honour again, but continued to turn up for training on a bicycle. Making his debut for Belgium in Sweden, still an eighteen-year-old, he calmly wrote postcards in the hotel where another might have been shaken by nerves. Temperament was always one of Van Himst's great strengths. Though his height and fine physique well equipped him to be a centre-forward, he was always prone to drop behind the line of attack, and it was not surprising that in due course he should become first a striking inside-forward, then withdraw to midfield. He had the pace, skill and force, however, often to break through to add to his many goals. He did much to get Belgium to the Finals of the World Cup in 1970 – though he had a curiously disappointing tournament in Mexico – and to the Finals of the European Nations Cup, two years later. Joining the Anderlecht club when he was not even ten years old, he stayed with them until the end of season 1974–5, where he distressed them by joining their rivals, Racing White, for a season. But no player had done more to keep Anderlecht in the forefront of European football over the previous fifteen years.

Obdulio Varela (Uruguay). The great hero of Uruguay's decisive win over Brazil in Rio in the 1950 World Cup, the huge Varela played then as an attacking centre-half. When Brazil threatened to overwhelm the Uruguayans, Varela it was, though now thirty-three years old, who not only inspired the Uruguayan defence to hold out, but began surging forward to carry the battle to the opposition. Four years later, in Switzerland's World Cup, he still looked a magnificent player. His first cap had been won as an inside-left back in 1940 when he scored three goals against Brazil. When he retired, he was given a job in the Montevideo Casino.

Vavà (Brazil). Born in Recife, which was also his first club, on 12 November 1934, his real name Edvaldo Isidio Netto, Vavà was Brazil's decisively effective centre-forward in their victorious World Cup tournaments of 1958 and 1962, scoring three goals in the two finals. In Stockholm in 1958 he closed in fast, twice, to convert centres from Garrincha (q.v.) in the first half, and in Santiago in 1962 he was on hand to score when Schroiff, the Czech goalkeeper, dropped the ball. Similarly, he had swooped to score against England in Viña del Mar when Garrincha's free kick bounced off Springett's chest, and he notched two more goals against Chile in the semi-final, both of them headed. He was a strong, quick, brave player, a great swooper on to half chances. Playing for Vasco da Gama from 1951 till after the 1958 Final – which was his seventeenth international game – he spent three seasons with Atletico Madrid, returned to Brazil in 1961 to play for Palmeiras of Sao Paolo and, somewhat unexpectedly but most successfully, forced his way back into the team again.

Berti Vogts (West Germany). An outstanding attacking fullback, an excellent marker and tackler, always eager to come forward, the blond Vogts won his seventy-third West German cap on the occasion of the 1976 European Nations Cup Final in Belgrade, having made his debut for West Germany against Yugoslavia in Belgrade on 3 May 1967. He took part in the 1970 World Cup in Mexico when West Germany reached the semi-finals, but briefly lost his place after a long run in the national team when it won the Nations Cup in Brussels in 1972. By 1974, however, he was reinstalled, and had an excellent World Cup, surviving an uneasy start in the Final in Munich, when he was given the daunting job of marking Johan Cruyff. With Borussia Munchengladbach he has won the Bundesliga and the UEFA Cup. He was born on 30 December 1946.

Bernard Vukas (Yugoslavia). A little blond left winger or inside-forward – he even played on the right wing in Rio for Yugoslavia in the 1950 World Cup – Vukas had one of his most notable games when called up at the last moment to play for the Rest of Europe against Britain in Belfast. That was in August 1955, and Vukas scored three of Europe's four goals. He had also played for Europe in the 4–4 draw against England at Wembley in October 1953. Born on 1 May 1927, his chief club was Hajduk of Split, but in 1957 he went for a spell to make some money with Bologna, in the Italian Championship. He had speed, control, an excellent shot.

Willy Waddell (Scotland). First capped on the right wing for Scotland in a wartime international at Hampden Park on 18 April 1942, Waddell helped Scotland to end a long run of failures against England with a 5–4 win. His international career extended another dozen years. His debut for Rangers was made in August 1938 at Highbury in a friendly against Arsenal. Waddell, still in his teens, scored the only goal of the game. He was a leading member both of the Rangers team which won two Cups and the League in 1948–9, the Cup and League double in 1952–3, an outside-right of power, pace and determination with a fierce right-footed shot. On retirement he became manager of Kilmarnock, whom he took to the Championship, most resourcefully and unexpectedly, in 1965. After some years as a journalist on the Scottish *Daily Express*, he became manager of Rangers in 1969, and stepped up to the position of General Manager a few years later.

Billy Walker (England). When Clem Stephenson (q.v.) left for Huddersfield Town, the mantle of strategist of the Aston Villa team descended on Billy Walker, and was worn with consummate success. Alan Morton (q.v.), the illustrious Scottish winger, called Walker the best inside-left he ever played against, Charlie Buchan (q.v.), no mean inside-forward himself, put Walker in his best post-1925 team. Idolized at Villa Park, and later a manager who won the Cup with two different clubs – Sheffield Wednesday in 1935, Nottingham Forest in 1939, after twenty years at Trent Bridge – Walker was the son of a well-known Wolves full-back. Born in Wednesbury, he scored prolifically as a centre-forward in Walsall schools football, signed pro for Villa in June 1919, 'made' two England left-wingers in Houghton and Dorrell, played sixteen times for England himself, a splendid captain and general.

Bobby Walker (Scotland). 'You would think,' said Jacky Robertson, his Scottish international contemporary, 'that Bobby had eight feet. You go to tackle him where his feet were, but they're away when you get there.' Walker's colossal skill made him one of the great Scottish inside-forwards before the Great War, even though he lacked speed – a traditional Scottish forward, perhaps. He twisted and turned past tackles, seldom to better effect than when Scotland beat England 2–1 in 1903 at Sheffield. His habitual inclination of the head, his apparent stiffness, belied the footballer he was. He won twenty-nine Scottish caps, spent his career with Heart of Midlothian, and produced a son who was as good an inside-forward as he.

Tommy Walker (Scotland). Bobby's son, and an inside-right of consummate quality, subtle, thoughtful, exact, a goal scorer as well as a maker of goals, winner of so many Scottish honours that in one wartime match at Hampden against England the whole Scotland team wore jerseys lent by Walker; though Walker was not playing. He himself spent much of the war in India with the Royal Air Force. Twenty-one times (including the war) capped for Scotland, he made his debut for them in 1932 and played 262 League games for them. After the war he joined Chelsea, for whom he had played as a guest, for two and a half years, returning to Hearts, with whom he became a successful manager. Won the first of his five full home international caps in season 1934–5.

Fritz Walter (West Germany). An admirable inside-forward, West Germany's impressive captain when they won the World Cup in 1954, Fritz Walter was strongly built, highly skilled, a strong shot and a fine user of the ball. A wartime paratrooper, he would not fly after the war, so shocked was he by the death of a comrade. Born in Kaiserlautern and always a member of the local club, he won the first of his sixty-one caps for Germany in 1940 on 7 July in Frankfurt as a centre-forward, scoring three out of nine goals against Rumania. On 1 September he got two out of thirteen against Finland. He was still in the team at inside-left when, on 22 November 1942, Germany beat Slovakia for what was to be their last international for exactly eight years. The ensuing period had done nothing to blunt Fritz Walter's edge, and he was joined now in the international team by his brother Otmar, a lively centre-forward. Each scored twice when Austria were memorably defeated 6–1 in the 1954 World Cup semi-final in Basel. Fritz's were penalties, but he was involved in all six. He was now thirty-three, but his strategy and general influence helped Germany to gain a famous victory in the Final against Hungary. He was prominently there once more in the World Cup of 1958 in Sweden, but a very severe foul by Parling in the semi-final against Sweden put him out of the third place match, and he did not play for Germany again. In his extraordinary, eighteen-year career with the German national team, he scored thirty-three goals.

Billy Wedlock (England). Nicknamed 'Fatty' or 'Smiler', this Bristol City player was one of the most renowned attacking centre-halves of the pre-Great War era, winning twenty-six caps. Born close to the City ground, he helped them to win the Championship of the Second Division in 1906, the Cup Final three years later. 'Wedlock was almost a freak footballer,' wrote Ivan Sharpe. 'There will never be another quite like him. He bounded about like an indiarubber man. He followed the forwards in the desirable, old-fashioned way, yet was back in defence when the ball came. He bobbed and bounced all over the place, smiling through.' First capped against Austria in 1908, his international career extended till 1914.

John White (Scotland). White died a pitifully early death when struck by lightning, sheltering on a golf course under a tree in the summer of 1964, on 21 July. He was still, at the time, one of the best, most graceful, most subtle inside-forwards in Britain, a beautifully accurate crosser of the ball from either wing, with an unusual gift for drifting unnoticed into telling positions. He had a wraith-like swerve, fine balance, unusual vision. Born at Musselburgh, he began his professional career with Alloa, joined Falkirk, was first capped for Scotland with them at centre-forward and inside-forward in 1959, joined Tottenham Hotspur that year, for £20,000, and for a time played on the right wing. The following season he, Danny Blanchflower (q.v.) and Dave Mackay were the motor and inspiration of the Spurs team which became the first this century to win the League and Cup double. Standing only 5 feet $7\frac{1}{2}$ inches, weighing just over 10 stone, never unfair or aggressive, White prevailed through sheer quality. His death was an infinite waste of a rare talent.

Faas Wilkes (Holland). Inside-left for the Rest of Europe in Glasgow against Britain in May 1947, the tall, lean Wilkes, a master of close control, was the inspiration of Johan Cruyff (q.v.) and perhaps the most accomplished of all Dutch players before him. Born in Amsterdam on 23 October 1923, it was the Xerxes club of Rotterdam with whom he emerged. In 1949 he was transferred to Internazionale of Milan, spent three years there, played with success for Valencia in Spain, and finished his career in Holland, where professional football was at last permitted.

Bert Williams (England). An admirable successor to Frank Swift (q.v.) and England's first World Cup goalkeeper in Chile in 1950, Bert Williams took some time to settle in the international team. Matches against France in London and

Paris played a strangely salient part in his career. In May 1945 he made his debut for England while still playing for Walsall, where he had been expertly coached by Harry Hibbs (q.v.). That was against France at Wembley, when the French surprisingly pulled the game out of the fire 2–2. Williams had made his name playing for the Royal Air Force representative team. Later that year he joined Wolverhampton Wanderers for £3,500, then a record fee for a goalkeeper. In May 1946 he was recalled to the England goal against France in Paris, England lost 2–1, and Williams was bundled into the net for one of the goals by Jean Prouff. Another three years, and it was May 1949, England against France in Paris, and a first full cap for Williams. Scarcely had the game begun than he dropped the ball and France scored, but he recovered to play splendidly, England won 3–1, and Williams was first choice for the next few years, winning in all twenty-four caps, plus those first two against France and a 1945 Victory international against Wales. His astonishing gymnastics robbed Italy of a deserved victory in the fogs of White Hart Lane, Tottenham in November 1949, and he should surely have played in the World Cup of 1950 rather than the demoralized Merrick, shattered by letting in thirteen Hungarian goals in two games, and badly at fault in the quarter-finals against Uruguay. Williams in fact was recalled the following season, and went on to add another five caps to his total. Born in the Midlands at Bradley, blond and well built, the fastest sprinter on Wolves's books in his day, he won both Cup and League medals with them.

Ray Wilson (England). England's tough, mobile, versatile left-back when they won the 1966 World Cup, Wilson in that period stayed blessedly free from the injuries which so often hampered him. Born at Shirebrook, near Mansfield, he developed with Huddersfield Town under the eye of another famous Town full-back, Roy Goodall (q.v.), with whom he disagreed over matters of style; Wilson held off where Goodall would have gone in. Wilson began as a left winger, which was easy enough to deduce from his adventurous play. He won his first cap for England in 1960 against Scotland at Wembley, and eventually brought that total to sixty-three, even though injury put him out of the team in 1960–61 and frustrated him on many other occasions. He played in the World Cup of 1962 in Chile, joined Everton in 1964, received his last caps in 1968, and was as much missed for his ebullient good humour as for his prowess on the field.

Vivian Woodward (England). An inside-right or centre-forward who always remained an amateur, Woodward was the equal of any of the England professionals of his epoch. Playing for England on twenty-seven occasions, including the tours of South Africa and Australia, he gained all but two of those honours while with Tottenham Hotspur. Born near Kennington, he modelled himself on G. O. Smith (q.v.) and like Smith was something of a triumph of mind over matter, for he was a slight man and, though good in the air, had little force behind his shots. Off the field, he was interested in pouter pigeons, fishing and photography. His demeanour endeared him to all who played with him; once, after a North–South game he was asked what his expenses were; and claimed 1s. 6d., $7\frac{1}{2}$ p in today's currency. He captained the United Kingdom team which won the Olympic football tournaments of 1908 and 1912 in London and Stockholm, served as a Captain in the Footballers' Battalion in the Great War, but was sadly lost to the game in later years.

Billy Wright (England). England's record holder of international caps with 105 till Bobby Charlton (q.v.) overtook it, Wright was like Moore, a blond English half-back who captained the team, but he was small where Moore was tall, began as an inside-left and perhaps played his best football for the team as a centre-half. His jumping was remarkable, and he regularly went higher than much taller centre-forwards. Born at Ironbridge, he went to Wolverhampton Wanderers as a fourteen-year-old and was nearly turned down for being too small. Fortunately for Wolves they kept him, for he captained them in the ensuing years to success in Cup and League. England first picked him as an inside-left against Belgium at Wembley in January 1946, but an injury to Frank Soo allowed him to drop to his favoured position of right-half. There he stayed to play in the 1950, 1954 and 1958 World Cups. It was in Berne, against Switzerland, in the 1954 competition that England moved him from wing-half to stopper with such success, and there is little doubt that this prolonged his international career. He was just as effective, and exuberant, in 1958, in Sweden. A player of boyish enthusiasm, high morale and sturdy defensive qualities, he managed Arsenal in the 1960s, then after leaving Highbury in 1965 went into sporting television in the Midlands.

Lev Yachine (Russia). As imposingly tall as his predecessor in the Moscow Dynamo and Russian goal, Khomich, was squat, Lev Yachine played with varied success in three World Cups, had a glorious forty-five minutes for the Rest of the World against England at Wembley in 1963, and was generally esteemed the best keeper of his time. Born in Moscow in 1929, he played ice hockey, basketball, volleyball, and was a diver and an athlete. The blond Bulgarian goalkeeper Sokolov was, he says, the player who inspired him with his daring rushes out of goal. In later years Yachine deplored the prevalence of the packed defence, which made life so hard for goalkeepers. His own secret, he thought, was 'to observe the opponent'. He left school at fourteen and worked in an aircraft factory before becoming a full-time footballer. He himself has said he was especially in form in the Olympic football tournament of 1956 in Melbourne, which Russia won, and in the 1958 World Cup series when they eliminated England. He was considerably less happy in the 1962 series, when a couple of most uncharacteristic lapses on long shots allowed Chile to score a surprising win in the quarter-final at Arica. In the 1966 World Cup he was blamed by his team manager for his play against West Germany in the lost semi-final at Everton; which seemed monstrously unfair after his agility and courage had for so long kept Russia in the game. Black jerseyed and, it sometimes seemed, possessed of an endless reach, he was a formidable goalkeeper to come up against; but he was also one of the most sporting players imaginable. On retirement, he remained with Dynamo as a coach.

Zagalo (Brazil). Real name: Mario Jorge Lobo Zagalo. An outside-left of remarkable lung power, Zagalo's exceptional stamina was Brazil's 'secret weapon' in their World Cup successes of 1958 and 1962. Endlessly dropping back, endlessly surging forward, able, in the 1958 Final, both to head out from beneath his own bar and to score the fourth Brazilian goal, he was more valuable still when Pelé dropped out in 1962. His selfless running, his deadly short centres, made Brazil's 4-3-3 effective and anything but negative. Zagalo has always been known as 'lucky', yet in fact he had a difficult initiation with Flamengo of Rio; a city to which his family moved from the North East when he was eight months old. Previously he played for the America club, but at Flamengo the fans did not warm to his cerebral, unspectacular play. Even after the 1958 World Cup, there were those who would have preferred to see Pepe, the Santos left winger, chosen, and there was doubt about Zagalo's choice in 1962 right up to the last moment. Luckily for Brazil, chosen he was. 'I wept,' he said. On returning from Sweden in 1958, he was transferred to Botafogo, managing both them and his previous club, Flamengo. Then in March 1970 he took over a demoralized Brazilian World Cup side; and won the trophy with them in Mexico. In West Germany in 1974 he'd lost too many star players to repeat the feat, but his team did reach the final pools. Born in 1931.

Ricardo Zamora (Spain). How ironic that Zamora, finest goalkeeper ever to play for Spain, hero alike of the 1920, 1924 and 1928 Olympic tournaments and the 1934 World Cup, should fail so wretchedly on his only visit to England, foundering in the Highbury mud on a winter's day of 1931, letting through two soft early goals, and eventually another five! 'He says that tonight in Madrid he is nothing,' said an interpreter afterwards to the English centre-forward Dixie Dean (q.v.) who replied roughly, 'Tell him he's nothing here, either.' But in fact Zamora was a great goalkeeper, forty-seven times capped for Spain, bold and gymnastic, winning thirty-one consecutive caps, letting in a mere twenty-seven goals in his first thirty-four internationals. His debut for Spain was made in the Antwerp Olympiad of 1920, he was splendid four years later in Paris, and eight years later in Amsterdam. Against a ruthless Italian attack in the semi-final of the 1934 World Cup in Florence he was wonderfully defiant; the Italians were held 1–1 after extra time, Zamora was fouled when the equalizer was scored, and so ill used that he couldn't play in the return which Italy won 1–0. Playing at first for Espanol then the other Barcelona club, Barcelona themselves, Zamora joined Real Madrid for a record 150,000 pesetas (then £6,000) fee in 1930. Later he became team manager of Spain, while his son was a First Division goalkeeper.

Branko Zebec (Yugoslavia). A footballer of astonishing versatility, good enough to play for the Rest of Europe against England at Wembley in 1953 on the left wing, and later to become Yugoslavia's centre-half. One can think of only Jack Froggatt of England in such a context of change. Zebec, born in 1929, played at outside-left and centre-forward for Yugoslavia in the 1954 World Cup in Switzerland, scoring his team's goal from the latter position in a memorable 1–1 draw in Lausanne. Tall, strong, a fine shot, excellent in the air, the transition to centre-half in the autumn of 1955 was instantly successful. Born in Zagreb, he originally joined the Gradjanski, and from the age of twelve benefited from the coaching of a celebrated Hungarian, Marton Bukovi. His next club was Locomotive Zagreb, but Army service took him to Belgrade where he joined Partizan, the military club, where he began a noted partnership with Stefan Bobek, the inside-left of the national team. Pace, force and a devastating left-footed shot soon made Zebec a star, and he had odd games at centre-half as early as 1953. In 1959 he joined Red Star Belgrade, having in 1958 played all three World Cup games for Yugoslavia in Sweden as a centre-half. One hesitates to refer to him as a stopper, so neat was his footwork, so good his distribution. He won sixty-five international caps, then went to West Germany where in due course he became a manager.

Zico (Brazil). Zico became the new hope of Brazilian football in season 1975–6, when he was incorporated into the team, having shown splendid form for Flamengo of Rio as a 'tactical' centre-forward, rather after the manner of Tostao (q.v.). Like Tostao he plays particularly well with his back to the goal, and again like Tostao he is relatively small. When Brazil played in the American Bicentennial Tournament of 1976 Zico was actually in midfield; he prefers to have more space if he can. One of several footballing brothers, of whom Edu, the winger, has teamed with him at Flamengo, Zico was once exceedingly fragile, but a course of weight lifting and steroids improved his physique. He owes much to indoor football; his extreme quickness, his fast reactions, are said to derive from it. Zico, twenty-three at the time of the American tournament, is also noted for his remarkable, swerving free kicks.

Zito (Brazil). It made an immense difference when Zito displaced Dina at right-half in the Brazilian World Cup team of 1958, in their third game, at Gothenburg, against Russia. Zito was the ideal, classical wing-half to partner Didì (q.v.) in the two-man midfield of the Brazilian 4-2-4 formation, a novelty then in international football. Fluent and strong, he could win the ball as well as distribute it. He could also score goals, as he would show in the 1962 World Cup Final against the Czechs in Chile when he headed in Amarildo's centre from almost under the bar to put Brazil 2–1 ahead. Born in 1933, he won his tenth international cap in that 1958 Final, while with Santos, Pelé's club, he was a winner of the Intercontinental Cup of 1962 and 1963, against Benfica and Milan. His real name is José Eli Miranda, his native town is Roseira in Sao Paolo state. He started as an amateur with the local team of that name, turned professional with Taubate, and thence moved to Santos. His original intention was to become a teacher and he initially joined Roseira simply to keep fit.

Zizinho (Brazil). His real name is Tomaz Soares da Silva and he was one of the most exciting forwards of the 1950 World Cup, when Brazil ran riot in the final pool to score seven against Sweden, six against Spain; but lost to Uruguay. Zizinho's dazzling control, his imagination and his suppleness made him at times irresistible. He made up an astonishing trio of inside-forwards with Ademir and Jair and he linked perfectly with the right-half Bauer. Born at Niteroi in the State of Rio on 14 September 1921, he first played for Carioca of Niteroi, then Byron, then for Flamengo of Rio, winning numerous medals, and ending his career with another Rio club, Bangu. In 1956, Brazil actually recalled him for a time to the colours.

Dino Zoff (Italy). A goalkeeper of great talent and huge dedication, Zoff kept the Italian goal inviolate for 1,143 minutes, till a Haitian forward called Sanon at last beat him in Munich in the 1974 World Cup. He hadn't played in the 1970 one, being kept out of the team by the reliable Albertosi, although he had helped Italy to win the European Nations Cup of 1968. Zoff was born in the North East of Italy at Mariano del Friuli on 28 February 1942, kept goal from his schooldays, turned professional with the Udinese club, once a famous First Division team, and made his debut in that championship in 1961. Mantova signed him in 1963, Naples in 1967, Juventus of Turin shelled out a huge fee for him plus their own goalkeeper Carmignani in 1972. With them he has won championship medals and played in the 1973 European Cup Final. An admirable positional player, highly agile, with an extremely magnetic pair of hands, Zoff at his best was probably the leading European goalkeeper of the mid 1970s.

About the Author

Brian Glanville is football correspondent of the *Sunday Times*, for whom he has covered every World Cup since 1958. Wrote and helped to edit GOAL! the prize-winning film about the 1966 World Cup. Author of fifteen novels and four books of short stories, among them *The Rise of Gerry Logan* and *The Dying of the Light*, novels about soccer stars. He still plays left-back for Chelsea Casuals F.C. on Sundays.

Other Puffins by Brian Glanville

Puffin Book of Football

A book which gives a clear, objective account of how
soccer came to be what it is today; how a game which
grew up in the English Public Schools has been brought
to Europe, America, Africa and Asia. It describes simply
and understandably, with diagrams and pictures, the growth
of tactics from the old five-forward game, through the
third-back formation, to the 4-2-4, 4-3-3 and sweeper
systems of today. We follow the development of English
club football as well as the history of the World Cup, and
every reader should derive a deeper interest in and
understanding of the game, how it has developed, what it
has become, and what may or may not happen to it in the
future.

Goalkeepers are Different

Brian Glanville is a novelist and sports journalist who
really knows his subject from the inside, and the result is
a fascinating glimpse into the world of the professional,
from early days as a club apprentice to the exhilarating
heights at the top of the tree. A gripping and fast-moving
book, as good as a football game.

Some other Puffins you might enjoy

The Puffin Soccer Quiz Book

David Prole

National teams and international clubs; Leagues and Cups; famous players and managers in Britain, Europe and the rest of the world; the vital winning goals and the fantastic saves – you'll find all these, and many more, in this super quiz book. There are lots of questions specially designed to test your knowledge of the game.

The Goalkeeper's Revenge

Bill Naughton

Thirteen stories about boys – including boys who fish, fight, play football, go to hospital, or apply for their first jobs.

Pete

Alison Morgan

'We do not want our school represented abroad by a gang of shoplifters,' said the headmaster, and that was that. Unfair though it was, Pete's trip to Germany was off, but suddenly an idea came to him that made it seem like the best luck he'd ever had ...

The Eighteenth Emergency

Betsy Byars

Benjie and Ezzie had often discussed what they would do if an octopus or a crocodile attacked them – but whatever is Benjie to do in the worst emergency of all, when Hammerman, the biggest boy in the school, is asking for a fight?

If you have enjoyed reading this book and would like to know about others which we publish, why not join the Puffin Club? You will be sent the club magazine, *Puffin Post*, four times a year and a smart badge and membership book. You will also be able to enter all the competitions. For details of cost and an application form, send a stamped addressed envelope to:

The Puffin Club Dept A
Penguin Books Limited
Bath Road
Harmondsworth
Middlesex

and if you live in Australia, please write to:

The Australian Puffin Club
Penguin Books Australia Limited
P.O. Box 257
Ringwood
Victoria 3134